HIGHLAND SCRAMBLES NORTH

S/R MULLACH/RATH 2

LONG STROLL SUNS 3

SWANTING BUTTRESS FANNICHS

OICHOG RIB 3

NW RIB TOOLLACH 3

EAST RIDGE M/C/F 2

NW BUTT SLIOCH 2/3

HIGHLAND SCRAMBLES NORTH

Scrambles and Easy Climbs

including

Applecross, Assynt, Caithness, Carnmore, Coigach, Easter Ross, Fannaichs, Fisherfield, Foinaven, Gairloch, Glen Affric, Kintail, Torridon and the Outer Hebrides

Iain Thow

SCOTTISH MOUNTAINEERING CLUB
SCRAMBLERS' GUIDE

Published in Great Britain by The Scottish Mountaineering Trust, 2006

© The Scottish Mountaineering Club

ISBN 0 907521 88 6
A catalogue record for this book is available from the British Library

Front Cover: South Ridge of Mullach an Rathain, Liathach (Route 73)
Scrambler: Noel Williams (Photo Iain Thow)

Route descriptions of scrambles and climbs in this guide, together with their grades and any references to in situ or natural protection, are made in good faith, checked and substantiated where possible by the author. However, routes lose holds and are altered by rockfall, rock becomes dirty and loose and in situ protection deteriorates. Even minor alterations can have a dramatic effect on a route's grade or seriousness. Therefore, it is essential that scramblers and climbers judge the condition of any route for themselves, before they start. The authors, editors, friends and assistants involved in the publication of this guide, the Scottish Mountaineering Club, the Scottish Mountaineering Trust and Scottish Mountaineering Trust (Publications) Ltd, can therefore accept no liability whatever for damage to property, nor for personal injury or death, arising directly or indirectly from the use of this publication.

This guidebook is compiled from the most recent information and experience provided by the author, members of the Scottish Mountaineering Club and other contributors. The book is published by the Scottish Mountaineering Trust, which is a charitable trust. Revenue from the sale of books published by the Trust is used for the continuation of its publishing programme and for charitable purposes associated with Scottish mountains and mountaineering.

Production: Scottish Mountaineering Trust (Publications) Ltd
Diagrams: Mark Hudson and Jean Thomas
Maps: Noel Williams
Design concept: Curious Oranj, Glasgow
Typesetting, diagram and map graphics: Noel Williams
Colour separations: Core Image, East Kilbride
Printed & bound in Spain by Elkar, Bilbao

Distributed by Cordee, 3a DeMonfort Street, Leicester. LE1 7HD
(t) 0116 254 3579, (f) 0116 247 1176, (e) sales@cordee.co.uk

CONTENTS

MAPS & DIAGRAMS

INTRODUCTION

The North-West Highlands and the Outer Hebrides (or Western Isles) contain some of the best scrambling anywhere in Scotland. If you enjoy unfrequented rock on wild, rugged peaks then this is the place for you. The area is huge (the Cuillin would fit into it more than 100 times over), and as a result the routes are widely scattered and sometimes quite remote. Despite this most routes can be done from a road in a reasonable day (with the exception of some routes around Carnmore). At one extreme Lurg Mhor and Seana Bhraigh involve long days, while at the other there are routes suitable for an evening trip, especially around Gairloch. The vast majority are mountain routes with all that implies in the way of weather conditions, the possibility of some loose rock and the need to be able to navigate safely and competently. It is essential that anyone doing these routes carries and can use a map and compass.

This book describes both scrambles and easy rock climbs and is aimed at both experienced climbers on an off day and adventurous walkers looking for some added excitement. Most types of scrambling are represented here; there are towering buttresses, narrow ridges, huge slabs and tumbling streams. Some routes find the easiest way up a big face, others look for difficulty on outcrop-scattered hillsides. One thing that many of them have in common is length – these are big hills, and the valley floors are often close to sea level. The start of one route can't be reached at high tide!

In most cases descents have not been described, as virtually all the scrambles here finish on summits or hillsides from which there is an easy way off. This may be rough or pathless and it may be quite a long way, but the skills brought into play are those of navigation and map reading rather than scrambling.

The remoteness of some of the routes gives them an added seriousness, especially in the event of an accident or drastic change in the weather (not an unknown occurrence in these parts). Some routes involve river crossings which can be tricky or impossible in bad conditions, while in some places snow may linger late into June or arrive quite early in October. On the other hand the sheer size of the area means that at any given time weather conditions vary across the region, so it should be possible to find good conditions somewhere. It should always be remembered, however, that all scrambling is potentially dangerous – **moving unroped in exposed situations calls for extreme care and should not be taken lightly**. Even the easier routes can take you into impressive and serious positions. Allow a wide margin for error and always be prepared to retreat or traverse off if necessary. However, don't lose sight of the fact that scrambling should be fun!

Iain Thow
May 2006

ACKNOWLEDGEMENTS

Although this is the first guide dedicated to scrambles in the North-West Highlands and the Outer Hebrides many of the routes have been described or mentioned before in a variety of places, notably the SMC District Guides to the North-West Highlands, Northern Highlands, Western Highlands and the Islands of Scotland. Many of the harder routes are also described in the various editions of the Northern Highlands and Skye and the Hebrides Climbing Guides edited by Ian Rowe, Derwent Turnbull, Roger Everett and Andy Nisbet. Of the other routes, some are well known or obvious, but over a third have not been recorded before. This doesn't of course mean that nobody has climbed them and there are traces of passage in many places. This guide is dedicated to my unknown predecessors.

Most of these unrecorded routes have been selected by the simple expedient of walking past them and thinking 'that looks good' – an approach which has inevitably led to the occasional minor epic! This guide only scratches the surface of the huge amount of rock available and the scope for additional routes is huge. I hope that it inspires more people to go out and explore this amazing area and that they have as much fun doing so as I've had.

My thanks especially go to Noel Williams for doing the desktop publishing work, for technical advice, helpful suggestions and writing the geology and mountaineering history sections; to Mark Hudson for his marvellous crag diagrams and his enthusiasm; to Jean Thomas for the exquisite plant and animal drawings and to Ro Scott for writing the wildlife section.

Thanks for company on the routes and for posing for photographs go to George Archibald, Robin Chalmers, Chris Dodd, Terry Doe, Peter Duggan, Paddy Earle, Paula Gibson-Hamilton, Angela Gillespie, Bob Glover, Willie Jeffrey, Liz Jolley, Ben Lowe, Marco de Man, Richard Merryfield, Andy Morrison, Lucy Williams, Noel Williams, Russ Yurkow and a gentleman from Sheffield whose name I never discovered.

Helpful suggestions came from Andy Bluefield, Linda Henderson, Ben Lowe, Andy Nisbet, Ken Stewart, Andy Waring and Bill Wright. Peter Elford helped with the intricacies of digital photography and he, Gill Machrie and Marco de Man let me use various computers, scanners, card readers etc. Noel wishes to thank Maarten Krabbendam and Graham Leslie of BGS for commenting on the geology section. I'm very grateful to Peter Duggan for his careful proof-reading and helpful suggestions. My thanks also go to Richard Gilbert for reading and commenting on the text and for his obvious affection for the North West. I should also like to record my debt to the late Harry Griffin for inspiring me to go scrambling in the first place. Lastly my apologies to anyone I have inadvertently omitted.

GEOLOGY

The area covered by this guide has a complex but fascinating geology. A glance at the geological map (see inside back cover) allows a simple interpretation to be made – older rocks in the west pass into younger rocks in the east, but with a great swathe of Moinian metamorphic rocks in the middle. However, there is one important complication. A major structure called the **Moine Thrust** runs all the way down through the North-West Highlands.

Most of the best scrambles in this guide are situated to the west of the Moine Thrust on rocks which comprise the Hebridean terrane or 'foreland' area. The unique character of this part of the Highlands is largely due to its distinctive rocks. The geology of the region is so special that in 2004 an area comprising much of Sutherland and part of Wester Ross was recognised as a European Geopark – the first area in Scotland to be awarded this status.

Section through the North-West Highlands

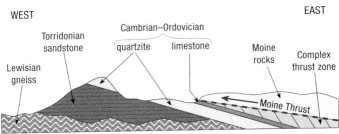

The structure of the North-West Highlands is summarised by the simplified cross-section shown above. The various rocks identified in this section will now be described in more detail, starting with the rocks of the foreland.

Lewisian

The oldest rock, found at the bottom of the pile, is a coarsely crystalline metamorphic rock known as Lewisian gneiss. It is some 3,000 million years old and one of the oldest rocks in Europe. The gneiss has pale/dark banding and is permeated by countless basic dykes, granite sheets and pegmatite veins which themselves have been metamorphosed to varying degrees.

Research is still unravelling the complex history behind this set of rocks, but three different metamorphic episodes are currently recognised. These are named after localities in Sutherland. The Scourian event dates from around 2,600 million years ago, the Inverian around 2,450 million years ago, and the Laxfordian around 1,800 million years ago. There then followed a long period of gradual uplift and erosion.

Lewisian rocks exposed in a road cutting near Scourie – showing older grey gneiss cut by black dykes, both of which are cut by younger pink granite veins.

The Outer Hebrides are built almost entirely from Lewisian rocks – hence the name. On low ground, being crystalline and impervious, the gneiss tends to form rugged, lochan-peppered moorland. Where it forms high ground it gives magnificent scrambling, among the best in this guide. In the Outer Hebrides the hills of Uig and North Harris give superb outings, as do the hills around Gairloch and Carnmore on the mainland. All of Ben Stack and the northern end of Foinaven are also built of this rock.

Torridonian

The basement of Lewisian gneiss was deeply eroded before the Torridonian sediments were laid on top. A pile of sandstones and conglomerates, at least 7km thick, was subsequently deposited on what was a very irregular land surface. On the slopes of Slioch above Loch Maree, for example, the Torridonian sandstone is seen to infill a deep valley in the Lewisian gneiss.

The Torridonian sediments were laid down some 1,200–1,000 million years ago, probably as extensive alluvial fans, and in wide channels of braided rivers. The rocks are too old to contain recognisable fossils, but microscopic traces of primitive life forms have been extracted from some beds. Despite its great age, the Torridonian sandstone to the west of the Moine Thrust zone has survived largely unchanged since it first formed. In other words, it has not been metamorphosed and so must have remained outwith any mountain building areas.

The Torridonian rock strata are mainly horizontal or gently inclined, and are cut by numerous vertical joints. They weather to produce terraced cliffs with steep chimneys and gullies, as well as rounded bastions and pinnacled ridges. Extensive outcrops of Torridonian sandstone occur throughout the North-West Highlands, making it the best exposed sedimentary formation in Britain. Being red in colour and well stratified it contrasts starkly with the contorted crystalline gneiss on which it rests. The extraordinary difference in character between these two rocks has been emphasised by erosion, and has produced some of the most dramatic mountain scenery in the country.

Suilven, though by no means the highest, is perhaps the best known and certainly one of the most spectacular of the peaks in the north-west. It consists of an isolated remnant of flat-lying Torridonian sandstone resting on a platform of Lewisian gneiss. The normal access route to the bealach on the summit ridge (see Route 19, p77) follows the line of a vertical fault. The main summit lies on the downthrown side of this fault.

Among the other peaks of Torridonian sandstone situated north of Ullapool are Cul Beag, Stac Pollaidh and Ben Mor Coigach. Several other peaks in that area (notably Quinag, Canisp and Cul Mor) are built of Torridonian strata with a capping of Cambrian quartzite. Farther south, mighty An Teallach is built largely of Torridonian sandstone. In Torridon itself, Beinn Alligin is built entirely from this rock, whilst Liathach and Beinn Eighe have minor and major caps of quartzite respectively. The Applecross hills are also carved from rocks of Torridonian age.

Although the coarse-grained sandstone gives good friction, the bigger faces tend not to be suitable for scrambling or rock climbing, because the thicker beds of sandstone are lacking in features and can prove surprisingly difficult to climb. The most common type of scramble on this rock is along ridge crests or easier angled buttresses, such as on An Teallach. On the south-east side of Fuar Tholl the Torridonian strata are inclined at a steeper angle than usual and so there give pleasant scrambling on delightful slabs.

Around 600 million years ago the Lewisian and Torridonian rocks were tilted north-westwards and eroded to a flat surface (peneplain) before the next group of rocks were deposited.

Cambrian and Ordovician

About 540 million years ago the sea began to transgress across the land, and eventually some 1,000m of marine sandstones and limestones were laid down on an almost level platform of Lewisian and Torridonian rocks. These new sediments were deposited along the southern margin of 'Laurentia' (North America and Greenland) in a broad shallow shelf enviroment.

Quartzites: The earliest deposits consist mainly of white, and sometimes pink, siliceous sandstones called quartzites. The upper part of the group includes a distinctive type of quartzite known as **Pipe Rock**. This contains numerous vertical tubes or pipes (10–20cm long) thought to represent the sand-filled burrows of worm-like organisms living in a beach environment.

Quartzite is a hard, well-jointed rock which breaks up readily into sharp-edged blocks. These blocks remain angular even after prolonged weathering and consequently are awkward to walk on. The rock is often badly shattered by freeze-thaw action and some impressive scree slopes flank the ridges of Foinaven for example, but where crags of sounder rock occur there is fine scrambling, notably on Creag Urbhard and Ruadh-stac Beag.

Foinaven and Arkle in the north of Sutherland are perhaps the best examples of mountains composed mainly of Cambrian quartzite. There the quartzite rests directly on Lewisian gneiss. However, for the most part the quartzite forms a cap or top tier to what are largely Torridonian sandstone mountains. The junction between sandstone and quartzite is easily seen, for example, running across the triple buttresses of Coire Mhic Fhearchair.

Limestones: As time went by the sandy sediments gave way to limestones and dolomites. These rocks are generally pale to dark grey in colour although some beds weather to a creamy yellow colour. Limestone tends to produce a greener sort of scenery with a more varied flora of great interest to botanists.

Although these beds are not extensive enough to form significant hills, around Inchnadamph and Elphin numerous caves have been created by streams sinking into the limestone – the longest over 2km in length. A very spectacular cave, Smoo Cave, lies on the north coast just east of Durness.

Fossils such as trilobites and brachiopods present in these Cambrian and Ordovician rocks can be matched with fossils found in Newfoundland and East Greenland. These are very different from the species found in the rest of Britain, because 'Avalonia' (England, Wales and southern Ireland) at that time lay further south on the opposite side of the Iapetus Ocean.

Some time after they were deposited the Cambrian and Ordovician strata were tilted gently to the south-east. This caused the underlying Torridonian sandstone to return to a more or less horizontal position.

Moinian

At roughly the same time as the Torridonian sediments were being deposited in rift valleys on land, a thick sequence of sands, silts and muds began to accumulate offshore (1,000–870 million years ago). These sediments were later caught up in a number of mountain building episodes caused by plate collisions, and were squeezed, folded and heated on a massive scale. The resulting group of rocks consist mainly of **psammites** (metamorphosed sandstones) and **pelites** (metamorphosed mudstones and shales) and are referred to as **Moine** rocks – named after the peninsula of A' Mhoine (the

Peat Bog) in northern Sutherland. These rocks form much of the Northern Highlands, but because they attract vegetation and generally form rather rounded hills they tend not to lend themselves to good scrambles or climbs. The Forcan Ridge of the Saddle is a notable exception.

In places the Moine and some of the foreland rocks were intruded by molten material, which cooled to form sills, dykes and stocks of various igneous rocks including syenite. Some of the intrusions have a distinctive porphyritic texture i.e. they contain prominent crystals (usually feldspar) set in a finer groundmass. Conspicuous sheets or sills can be seen within the Torridonian sandstone strata on the north-west side of Canisp and around Suilven's eastern top. Much of Ben Loyal is formed from a syenite pluton.

The Moine rocks we see today represent the eroded root of part of the once mighty Caledonian Mountain Chain, remnants of which can be traced from Spitzbergen down through Scandinavia, across the British Isles to Newfoundland and eastern North America. The Caledonian mountains, which at one time were probably comparable in character to the present day Hindu Kush and western Himalaya, were deeply eroded prior to the deposition of the next group of rocks belonging to the Devonian period.

The Moine Thrust Zone

A thrust is a low angled fault. The Moine Thrust itself is the highest of a series of thrusts which lie within a narrow belt of dislocated rocks known as the **Moine Thrust Zone**. The plane of the Moine Thrust slopes up gently towards the west-north-west. During the Caledonian mountain building episode about 430 million years ago, Moine metamorphic rocks were pushed a total of at least 100 kilometres west-north-westwards up onto the younger Cambrian and Ordovician quartzites and limestones. As a result of this large scale displacement the rocks immediately above the thrust plane were 'rolled out' and changed into a new rock called **mylonite**. Numerous 'chopped up' slices of quartzite and other foreland rocks are present within the thrust zone. In some localities (notably Glencoul) large slices of Lewisian gneiss were also brought up and thrust on top of younger quartzites.

Much controversy accompanied the early study of the rock sequence in the North-West Highlands, and some very eminent geologists – notably Murchison and Geikie – tried to insist that the Moine rocks were in normal stratigraphical sequence with the underlying Cambrian and Ordovician strata. Careful mapping by members of the British Geological Survey in the 1880s, however, demonstrated convincingly that older rocks had indeed been translated several tens of kilometres over younger rocks. This work culminated with the publication of an important memoir to the area in 1907. Such was the importance of these discoveries that in subsequent years geologists came from around the world to attend field excursions at Inchnadamph organised by Peach and Horne – two of the principal geologists who mapped the thrust structure for the Geological Survey.

The classic exposure of the Moine Thrust at Knockan Crag, near Elphin.
Dark Moinian rocks have been thrust over younger, cream-coloured limestones.

Anyone interested in understanding the landscape of the North-West Highlands is referred to two extremely well-illustrated publications *Northwest Highlands – a Landscape Fashioned by Geology*, and *Exploring the Landscape of Assynt* (listed under Further Reading). Both have been produced very much with the non-specialist in mind. The trail at Knockan Crag near Elphin, which visits a classic exposure of the Moine Thrust, is also strongly recommended.

Mention should also be made of two other important structures present in the area. The first is the eastward-dipping **Outer Isles Thrust**, which runs the full length of the Outer Hebrides, and manifests itself most clearly in the Uists as a line of hills with a west-facing scarp. The second is the **Great Glen Fault** – a tear fault most active around 430–400 million years ago – which forms the eastern boundary of the Northern Highlands area.

Devonian (and Mesozoic)

Following the Caledonian mountain building episode, the only significant deposits which survive in the Highlands are the conglomerates and flagstones of Devonian age (about 410–370 million years old), which outcrop extensively in the north and east.

Fossil fish, found at numerous localities from John o' Groats to the Black Isle, suggest that many of these sediments were laid down in a huge body of freshwater – the Orcadian Lake. The rocks generally form fairly featureless moorland, with Morven in Caithness being the most significant summit. The sandstone seacliffs around the north-east coast are especially scenic.

A narrow strip of much younger sedimentary rocks (of Jurassic age) outcrops on the south side of the Helmsdale Fault between Brora and Helmsdale. A metre-thick seam of coal was worked at Brora for many years.

Quaternary

The mountains we see in the North-West Highlands today were created by uplift which took place during the rifting process associated with the opening of the North Atlantic around 50 million years ago. However, the final moulding of these mountains was brought about mainly by the action of the huge ice sheets and glaciers which built up and melted away many times during the last two million years. Large quantities of rock were scooped out of the corries and glens. At times of maximum glaciation the area was completely covered by ice, but at other times the higher summits in the west remained exposed as **nunataks**.

During the most recent minor glacial episode 12,000 years ago (the Loch Lomond Stadial) ice built up principally where precipitation was greatest i.e. over western hills. A large ice cap extended from the Trossachs in the south to Torridon in the north. Further north many of the major peaks developed glaciers in their northern corries. A very obvious example of a terminal moraine can be seen, for example, below the north-eastern corrie of Beinn Dearg Mor – this is especially obvious when viewed in the right light from Sail Liath on An Teallach.

Freeze-thaw action occurred on summits exposed above the ice, and on ground surrounding glacial areas. Such periglacial conditions produced shattered bedrock (blockfield), scree, stone stripes and polygons, as well as debris showing signs of downslope movement or solifluction. For example, the frost-shattered quartzite ridge between Conival and Ben More Assynt points to these peaks being nunataks during the last major glaciation.

Remains found in the Bone Caves near Inchnadamph indicate that during milder inter-glacial episodes brown bear, Arctic fox, lynx, reindeer and wolf were roaming this part of Scotland. Other remains tell of the presence of polar bear during colder spells.

Where glaciers stagnated and melted away in places they left behind extensive **hummocky moraines**. One of the best examples of this sort of terrain can be seen in the glen behind the Ling Hut in Torridon. Its name, Coire a' Cheud-chnoic, means *Corrie of a Hundred Hills*.

Large rock slope failures also occurred where steep hillsides were no longer supported by valley glaciers. A superb example (best viewed from Sgurr nan Saighead) lies on the south-western flank of Beinn Fhada above Gleann Lichd, where an area of more than 3km^2 has moved downslope.

HUMAN HISTORY

With the exception of a narrow strip along the east coast of the mainland the North-West Highlands and Outer Hebrides are rough and rocky, ideal scrambling country but poor farming land – less than 10% of it has ever been used for crops. Thin acid soils mean that it has never been heavily settled, although there are scattered sites going back as far as the Mesolithic – the shell middens at the mouth of Strathnaver, for example. By 2000BC there were enough people in the area for the construction of the stone circles around Callanish in Lewis, the main circle being one of the most impressive prehistoric sites in the country, aligned to the extreme rising and setting points of the moon. In the Late Bronze Age the climate became colder and wetter, making farming even harder, and the arrival of the Celts with iron weapons meant more people chasing less cultivable land, leading to the construction of many small forts as people tried to protect what they had. The most spectacular of these are the brochs, tall tapering drystone towers unique to Northern Scotland. Dun Dornaigil below Ben Hope, Dun Carloway in Lewis and the two near Glenelg are good examples.

The rugged and indented coastline of the North-West means that until recently the sea was always the best highway, and while Lowland Britain was under Roman control tribes from the north of Ireland known as Scotti sailed across and settled here, bringing the Gaelic language. By the early 6th century they had set up a kingdom known as Dalriada with its heartland in modern Argyll but stretching much farther north. The bulk of the North-West was probably part of the Kingdom of the Northern Picts, centred on Inverness, although only half a dozen Pictish carvings have survived away from the east coast.

In 563 an Irish monk named Columba was exiled from Ireland and set up a community on the tiny island of Iona, close to Mull. This became the religious centre from which Scotland was converted to Christianity. Most of its early kings are buried there and it still exudes a sense of quiet peace and holiness today. Columba and contemporaries such as Maelrubha set up monasteries all over Scotland, and after the Scots King Kenneth MacAlpin took over the Pictish throne in 843 it is likely that their influence was important in enabling the Scots to absorb the much larger and more populous Pictish kingdom (although the wiping out of much of the Pictish nobility by the Vikings in 839 must have helped!).

The joint kingdom prospered and expanded southwards, but in doing so lost control of the west and north to the Vikings. The Isles were officially ceded to the wonderfully-named Norwegian king Magnus Barelegs in 1098. The Western Isles became Norse territory, ruled either from the Isle of Man, by the Earls of Orkney or by the Norwegian kings themselves. Place names such as Durness (deer headland) and Suainaval (hill of the pigs) are the result, with Norse/Gaelic hybrids such as Suilven (pillar mountain) reflecting a bilingual society. In 1156 a half Norse, half Gaelic chieftain named Somerled won a sea battle over the Norse King of Man (his brother-in-law) and gained control of the Inner Hebrides and the west coast. Somerled was killed in 1164, but from him descended the MacDonalds and MacDougalls who ruled the area for the next three centuries. Feuding continued with the Macleods, the descendants of the Vikings who still controlled Lewis, Harris and parts of Skye.

The last Viking Earl of Orkney died in 1231, and in 1263 a huge Norwegian expedition was scattered by a storm after a minor skirmish at Largs on the Ayrshire coast. The succeeding Norwegian king sold his rights over the area to the Scottish King Alexander II, but he died in an attempt to enforce them, and his successors were preoccupied with the threat from England. In the resulting power vacuum the descendants of Somerled styled themselves Lords of the Isles and presided over a sea-based empire with wide trading links and a thriving cultural life. They were effectively independent princes with their own court and laws, building castles such as Ardtornish and Dunscaith to emphasise their authority. A dispute over the Earldom of Ross led to an invasion of the east and a bloody defeat at Harlaw in Aberdeenshire in 1411, but it was not until John of the Isles signed an independent treaty with England that the Stewart kings decided to turn their theoretical overlordship into reality, and the Lordship was forfeited in 1494.

For the next 300 years it was the policy of the Scottish (and later British) Crown to neutralise the MacDonalds by building up the power of the Campbells in Argyll and the Mackenzies in Ross. They were aided in this by Clan Donald's talent for backing lost causes, notably those of the later Stuart kings, Charles I, James II and the Jacobite pretenders. The only actual fighting that took place in the North-West during this chaotic period was in 1719, when Spanish troops landed in Kintail and along with a force of Jacobites were defeated in a battle in Glenshiel, the Spanish retreating up the hillside and over Sgurr nan Spainteach. Bonnie Prince Charlie also had a brief acquaintance with the area while being pursued after Culloden, being sheltered in Coire Dho and in South Uist.

Throughout all these upheavals it is likely that for most people most of the time life was dominated by more domestic considerations. They lived in small settlements of a few families, raised cattle, grew oats and barley, fished, wove cloth and cut peat for fuel. The land was divided into strips, which were allocated to tenants on a yearly basis by lot (the runrig system), then the cattle were allowed onto the fields once the crops were harvested. In the summer the animals were grazed high on the hills, looked after from temporary shelters known as shielings, the remains of which can be seen in numerous places. In the autumn cattle which couldn't be fed over the winter were driven south to the markets at Crieff (and later Falkirk) and sold to provide a small monetary income in order to buy the things the communities couldn't make themselves. The droving trade reached its height in the 18th Century, when tens of thousands of animals were sold every year. The introduction of the potato in the 18th Century caused an increase in population, and the small raised potato beds known as lazybeds are still very prominent all over the west coast and islands.

The failure of the Jacobite rising of 1745 led to drastic consequences for the Highlands, initially due to the brutal reprisals carried out by the Duke of Cumberland, but more permanently as successive governments made a concerted attempt to eradicate Highland culture. Ironically they were aided in this by many of the chiefs themselves. Up to this time these had managed their land so as to maintain as many fighting men as possible, but once the Highlands were disarmed after Culloden their power depended on having money and influence in Edinburgh and London rather than men. The easiest way to obtain this was to evict the people, now an encumbrance, and let the land for sheep to Lowland shepherds, who could pay ten times the rent. In the century after Culloden tens of thousands were evicted and shipped, more or less unwillingly, to Canada and Australia, while many more went to swell the populations of Glasgow, Edinburgh, Dundee and Paisley. Popular myth (backed by the notorious case of Sutherland) has it that this was done by the English, but in most cases it was the clan chiefs themselves who carried out the Clearances, leaving the Highlands a largely empty land. During the late 19th century, the post-Balmoral fashion for sporting estates led to the replacement of sheep by herds of deer managed for shooting, leaving even fewer people.

The decline of the Gaelic language followed from the evictions, and now there are only around 80,000 native speakers, mainly in Skye and the Western Isles. The language is having something of a revival at present though, centred around Gaelic music, which has led to many younger people continuing to use the language after childhood. The building of new roads has made the area far more accessible, and tourism is by far the biggest employer, although fishing and crofting are still important and there are a few large employers, mostly on the east coast. The biggest changes of the last half century have been the damming of many lochs for hydro-electric schemes and the introduction of large scale forestry, especially in the eastern part of the area. At first most plantations were of imported Sitka spruce, which grows far faster than the native Scots pine, but the last few years have seen a promising trend for the planting of native species, notably in Glen Affric and Kintail. Despite its sad history, most of the North-West remains unspoiled wild mountain country, breathtakingly beautiful, and as aloof from the turbulent activities of man as it has ever been.

WILDLIFE

This chapter gives an introduction to the varied plant and animal life which may be encountered whilst tackling these scrambles in North-West Scotland. Because the scrambles are widely spread across the north-west mainland and the Western Isles, it is not possible to give a detailed guide to each locality – so this is more of a general introduction to the whole area. Also, the rocks most suitable for scrambling tend to be hard and stable, which makes them less conducive to plant growth than softer, more friable rocks. So, whilst a limited range of plant species will be encountered on the routes themselves, the approach to and descent from the scrambles offers a greater opportunity to observe some of the diverse plant and animal life for which the area is famous. The books listed under 'further reading' should be consulted for more detail on individual localities.

Different plant species are variously equipped to cope with the challenges of geology, climate and topography. The nature of the vegetation found at any particular place depends on the chemical composition and physical characteristics of the substrate, degree of exposure to wind, annual rainfall, duration of snow-lie and also the land management history. Biogeography also plays a part, with some common mainland species being completely absent from the Western Isles. We will start at sea level and work upwards through the major habitat types.

In North-West Scotland the coast is never far away, and sea views add greatly to the enjoyment of a day on the hill. Several plants of coastal habitats – **thrift** (or sea-pink), **sea plantain**, **scurvy grass** and **sea campion** – are also found in the mountains. Other cliff plants – the celery-like **Scots lovage** and the leathery **sea spleenwort** fern – are more strictly maritime. Conversely, because of the extreme severity of the climate, some plants found only at high altitudes in the south and east of the country (for example, the **yellow saxifrage** and **mountain avens**) descend to sea level in the north-west. These two species are not found at all in the Western Isles.

The cliffs of the north-west mainland and Lewis, with their spectacular offshore islands and stacks, form summer tenements for colonies of seabirds – **guillemots**, **razorbills**, **kittiwakes** and **fulmars**. These birds spend most of their lives at sea, only making landfall to breed. **Peregrine falcons** exploit this seasonal bounty, hunting along the cliffs to feed their own broods. On the north Sutherland coast, short cliff-top turf is studded in spring with the bluebell-like flowers of **spring squill** and, in a few places, the tiny **Scottish primrose**. The sheltered sea-lochs along rocky coastlines on either side of the Minch, with their thick fringe of **brown sea-weeds**, small salt-marshes and **yellow iris** beds, provide ideal habitat for **otters**. Further offshore, you may be lucky enough to spot a **minke whale** or pod of **bottle-nosed dolphins**, but **harbour porpoises** or **seals** (grey or common) are more likely.

Sandy bays, as at Sandwood, Oldshoremore and Clachtoll on the mainland, and the western seaboard of the Uists, support crofting landscapes with colourful displays of flower-rich machair (grassland on blown shell-sand) in summer. Burrowing animals such as **moles** (not in the Western Isles) and **rabbits** are restricted to these drier grassland areas. Both of these species are preyed upon by the **buzzard**, which is the commonest large bird of prey at lower altitudes. Any 'eagle' perched on a fence post or telegraph pole...is a buzzard! Another common bird of agricultural and moorland landscapes is the **hooded** ('hoodie') **crow** – a two-tone version of the more southerly carrion crow. Further inland, waders such as **lapwing**, **curlew**, **oystercatcher** and **redshank** nest in pastures and arable fields in the cultivated glens, but retreat to the coast in winter. The short, steep river systems of the western seaboard are generally low in nutrients and support species, such as the **freshwater pearl mussel** and **dipper**, which require clear, sediment-free water, as do the commercially-important populations of **Atlantic salmon** and **sea trout**.

Native woodlands are generally sparse in the North-West Highlands, and practically absent from the Western Isles. Their occurrence is limited by the restricted extent of mineral soils, extreme oceanic climate and long history of burning and grazing. **Oak** is a southern species which reaches its northern geographical limit in Assynt, where its growth is severely limited by the wind. These damp north-western oakwoods, as at Letterewe, are remarkable for their profusion of non-flowering plants – lichens, mosses, liverworts and filmy ferns – which thrive on the high humidity. Typical birds of these woods are the **redstart** and **wood warbler**. **Scots pine** is more at home on the colder north-facing slopes of Torridon and the west side of Loch Maree. These western pinewoods lack some of the 'typical' pinewood plant and bird species found further east, but the tinkling calls of tiny **goldcrests** may still be heard as they seek out insects among the foliage. Woods of **ash** and **hazel** are restricted to the calcareous soils of the Durness limestones, as at Kishorn. These woods have a rich ground flora, with **bluebell**, **dogs' mercury**, **sanicle** and in a few places the scarce **dark red helleborine** orchid.

In the extreme north, only the resilient **birch** forms extensive woodlands, such as those at Loch Stack. The **rowan** is equally resilient, but usually grows scattered amongst trees of other species, or clinging to the side of a sheltered gully high on the hill. **Eared willow** prefers the damper ground on lower slopes or in valley bottoms, where the banks of rivers and burns are lined with **alder**. Typical mammals of the mainland woods include the **pine marten** and **wildcat**, which were able to evade 19th Century persecution in their North-West Highland stronghold, due to the absence of the strict predator control found on the more easterly grouse moors. **Roe deer** are widespread but wary, most often seen as a white rump bouncing away into the undergrowth, accompanied by a gruff bark of alarm.

The combination of high rainfall and acidic rocks makes North-Western Scotland ideal for the growth of bogs, and the approach to many of the

Pine Marten

scrambles will involve a somewhat soggy walk-in. The colourful **Sphagnum mosses** which carpet the bog surface are also essential to its formation. Their growing-point is at the top and, as the lower parts die, the acidic water which they hold prevents decomposition, so that peat slowly accumulates. The oldest Lewisian rocks, found in the Western Isles and the mainland west of the Moine thrust, present a knobbly low-relief topography, with bogs and lochans occupying the hollows between bald rocky knolls. Here, familiar plants such as **heather** and **deer-grass** grow in combination with bog specialists which are well-adapted to the nutrient-poor, acidic and wet conditions. The carnivorous **sundews** and **butterworts**, which trap insects on their rosettes of sticky leaves, are found on bare peat and along the margins of pools and lochans. Below the water, **bladderworts** also pursue a carnivorous lifestyle, ensnaring small aquatic creatures in their tiny traps. Unfortunately, the combined efforts of all these carnivorous plants still fail to make much of a dent in the **midge** population! **Bog bean** and **bottle sedge** are 'emergent' plants – rooting on the loch floor but with leaves and flowers above the surface. These watery boglands provide excellent habitat for **damselflies** and **dragonflies**, including the spectacular **azure hawker**, which has its stronghold in the North-Western Highlands. Among the birds, the **greenshank** is similarly concentrated in the North-West, including the Western Isles, during the breeding season. The **golden plover** is more widespread, inhabiting drier moorlands and mountain tops as well as the bogs. Both species winter in coastal habitats. **Red-throated divers** nest on islands in the smaller peatland lochans, whereas their black-throated cousins prefer larger lochs. Some of the larger mainland lochs, such as Loch Sionascaig (Inverpolly), are home to the **Arctic charr**, a non-migratory member of the salmon family.

Intermediate between bog and moorland, wet heaths cover extensive areas in the north-west. Sphagnum mosses are still present, but occupy a smaller proportion of the surface. Heather and **cross-leaved heath** are the dominant dwarf shrubs, accompanied by deer-grass, **purple moor-grass**, **common cottongrass**, **bog asphodel** and **lousewort**. The aromatic **bog myrtle** prefers to grow where there is lateral water movement through the peat.

Where drainage is better and peat thinner, drier moorlands dominated by heather, **blaeberry** (bilberry) and **bell-heather** are found. Beneath the taller shrubs creep stems of **tormentil**, with its four-petalled yellow flower and **heath bedstraw**, bedecked with clusters of tiny white stars. Flowers of the **heath milkwort** may be white, blue or purple. Smaller evergreen shrubs such as the confusingly-named **crowberry**, **cowberry** and **bearberry** occur more sporadically. The upright branched stems of the **fir clubmoss** conceal spore-producing parts among their topmost leaves, whereas the creeping **stag's-horn clubmoss** produces conspicuous twin cones on a separate stalk. Under leggy heather, the tiny **lesser twayblade orchid**, with its paired leaves, may be found. More conspicuous flowers include those of the **common spotted orchid**, which can occur in a range of colours from almost pure white to dark blotched purple and, later in summer, the pale blue **devil's-bit scabious**. On drier knolls, low-growing **dwarf juniper**, **Arctic bearberry** and **mountain everlasting** are characteristic.

Red deer range over most of the moorlands in the North-West and the Western Isles, and deer stalking is an important part of the local economy. An Teallach and the hills of Kintail are renowned for their populations of **feral goats**. These shaggy beasts are the descendants of domestic goats allowed to run free in centuries past. Their exact antiquity is disputed. Of the smaller animals, **mountain hare**, **common lizard**, **common frog**, **adder** and **slow worm** can be found on the mainland moors, although all are absent from the Western Isles. A variety of impressively large moths and butterflies inhabit the moorlands and bogs. For much of the year, the hairy caterpillars and papery pupal cases are the most conspicuous evidence of the **northern eggar moth**. The velvety-brown adults take wing only in May and June. **Emperor moth** caterpillars are well-camou-

Feral Goat

Top: Dwarf Juniper   Left: Fir Clubmoss   Right: Alpine Clubmoss

flaged on their food-plant, heather, being green with a line of small pink dots resembling flower-buds. The adult moths have spectacular eyespots on both pairs of wings. In July the **dark green fritillary** butterfly is a powerful flyer across the drier moorlands, where its larvae feed on **violets**. The **large heath** is less conspicuous and, since cotton-grasses are its larval food-plant, tends to be found in boggier areas. Perhaps the commonest moorland bird is the **meadow pipit**, whose ground-level nest is a favourite target of the **cuckoo**. The **stonechat** and **whinchat** nest among shrubby vegetation whereas the **wheatear** chooses rocky or stony places. These small songbirds provide food for the **merlin**, our smallest moorland bird of prey. The **hen harrier**, which prefers lower, rolling moorlands as in the Uists, also takes larger prey items. Populations of **field voles**, although at lower densities than in grassland habitats, support mammal-eating predators such as the **short-eared owl**. Both species are absent from Lewis and Harris.

The sudden appearance of a green patch, in a predominantly brown moorland landscape, indicates an outcrop of base-rich rock. These are more frequent as small intrusions among the Lewisian rocks of the western seaboard and Western Isles than in the Torridonian and Moine rocks of the mainland interior. Along the Durness limestone outcrops which follow the Moine thrust northwards from Kishorn to Durness, more extensive species-rich calcareous grasslands occur. These present a colourful spectacle in early summer, with a proliferation of orchids, **common birds-foot-trefoil**, **eye-brights**, **wild thyme** and **fairy flax** in their short turf. Later in the season, the flowers of **frog orchid** and **grass of Parnassus** will appear, along with fertile fronds of the tiny fern, **moonwort**. Montane species such as mountain avens, **whortle-leaved willow**, **Alpine bistort**, **Alpine meadow-rue** and **Alpine cinquefoil** may be seen at relatively low altitudes on the limestone, most notably at Inchnadamph. Here, and at Kishorn and Durness, areas of bare limestone 'pavement' occur, where grazing-sensitive plants such as **wild garlic** and **holly fern** are able to survive in the shelter of deep cracks, or grykes, where water has dissolved away the rock. Seepages of alkaline water across the ground surface form calcareous 'flushes', where plants such as the **Scottish asphodel** (a smaller, paler relative of the bog asphodel), **black bog-rush**, yellow saxifrage, and the worm-like **hooked scorpion-moss** may be found. The limestone streams of Assynt provide a habitat for the **water vole**, now endangered in many places by the spread of introduced **American mink**. The alkaline lochs of Assynt and Durness support plants such as **mare's-tail**, **blue water-speedwell** and **stoneworts**, which cannot tolerate acid water.

On more acid soils, grasslands composed of **bents** and **fescues** may be poorer in flowers, but provide favoured grazings for red deer and domestic stock far up onto the hill. **Viviparous fescue**, in which the seeds germinate whilst still attached to the parent plant, shows adaptation to the harsh mountain conditions. The appearance of **Alpine lady's mantle**, dwarf **cornel** and **Alpine clubmoss**, signal that you are gaining altitude.

The plants most likely to be encountered on the scrambles themselves are either those with long taproots, which can anchor themselves in rock crevices, or those which grow in pockets of soil accumulated on ledges. The first group include thrift, familiar from its alternative seashore habitat, the succulent **roseroot** and pink-flowered **moss campion**. Those growing on ledges include the tall perennials such as **globeflower**, **meadowsweet**, **wild angelica**, **greater woodrush**, **wood cranesbill**, **goldenrod**, **northern bedstraw**, **water avens** and **melancholy thistle**. These plants are generally

A Thrift
B Roseroot
C Bearberry
D Alpine Lady's Mantle

E Raven
F Common Sandpiper
G Golden Eagle
H Ring Ouzel

palatable to sheep and deer, and benefit greatly from the protection offered by inaccessible ledges, where they grow and flower with a luxuriance unequalled in grazed situations. Higher up, real mountain specialists such as **Alpine saw-wort** and, in a few mainland localities on the richer rock types, small remnant populations of mountain willows, including **downy willow**, **woolly willow** and **net-leaved willow**, can be found in similar places.

The water of most hill lochs and lochans is acidic and nutrient-poor, supporting a limited but characteristic range of plants, including **shoreweed**, **water lobelia**, **water horsetail**, bottle sedge, **white water-lily** and, in the most acidic, **awlwort**. Some hill lochs have populations of **brown trout** which have survived in isolation since the last ice-age. Others have been augmented by stocking. The plaintive call of the **common sandpiper** characterises the hill lochans in spring, when it arrives to nest by the waterside.

Where acidic water seeps out of the ground, spring-heads with the bright green **fountain apple-moss** and delicate starry saxifrage dot the hillsides. Up in the corries, patches of scree may support populations of the appropriately-named **parsley fern**, whose crinkled leaves resemble the garden herb. Where snow lies late into the summer, a distinctive vegetation develops, with **mat-grass**, and on the mainland only, the clover-like **Sibbaldia** and **dwarf cudweed**. The high corries provide secure nesting sites for **golden eagles** and **ravens** and secluded pastures for calving red deer hinds. On the mainland the hill **fox** makes its dens in the high rocks, and may occasionally be surprised foraging (or even sleeping) in broad daylight. Foxes are absent from the Western Isles. The **ring ouzel** is another summer visitor, and its fluting song epitomises the high places.

On completing your scramble you may emerge onto a windswept ridge or plateau. Here the vegetation will typically (on the mainland – many of these plants are absent from the Western Isles) consist of low-growing woody shrubs such as **dwarf willow**, **mountain azalea**, and cushion plants including moss campion and **mossy cyphel**. The spindly **three-leaved rush**, **spiked wood-rush** and **stiff sedge** stand vertical, defying the wind. On broader ridges and plateaux, the **woolly fringe-moss** forms extensive grey carpets, interspersed with plants of Alpine clubmoss and **Icelandic reindeer-moss** (which, perversely, is not a moss but a lichen). On the more fractured and angular rock types, for example the Torridonian sandstones and Cambrian quartzites, the summits and ridges may appear practically bare of vegetation. But a closer look reveals an intricate crazy paving of tiny **lichens** covering the rock surface.

Of the birds whose breeding is restricted to the high tops, **ptarmigan** are widespread in the North-West Highlands. They remain all year round, relying on their changeable plumage for camouflage (white in winter, mottled brown in summer). **Snow bunting** and **dotterel** have a more limited breeding distribution, using only the highest rocky summits and mossy plateaux respectively. All three species are absent as breeders from the Western Isles, but snow buntings visit in winter, to forage along the Hebridean coastline.

MOUNTAINEERING HISTORY

For many years remoteness, poor roads and a moist climate combined to put off all but the most determined travellers from visiting North-West Scotland. The exploration of the mountains in the Northern Highlands and the Outer Hebrides has therefore been slower and more sporadic than elsewhere in Britain. Only a brief outline of events is given here. Fuller details of the early pioneers can be found in Ian Mitchell's book, *Scotland's Mountains before the Mountaineers*. For more recent ascents see current SMC climbing guides.

Hunters, Cartographers and Soldiers
1250 The naming of Coire Mhic Fhearchair (*corrie of Farquar's son*) suggests that Farquar MacIntaggart's son, William, visited the corries of Mullach Coire Mhic Fhearchair and Beinn Eighe around this time.

1580s Fionnladh Dubh (*Black Findlay*) a famous archer and forester of Glen Cannich shoots an intruder dead with a bow and arrow, and dumps the body in the loch below the summits of Carn Eige and Mam Sodhail. He is credited with the ascent of nearby Beinn Fhionnlaidh (*Findlay's Hill*) above Loch Mullardoch – the first recorded bagging of a Munro beyond the Great Glen.

1590s Timothy Pont makes an extended cartographic study of Scotland. His sketches of the mountains suggest that he ascended some way up the hills. After his death his work was incorporated in the famous Blaeu Atlas.

1654 Blaeu's *Atlas Novus* is published in Amsterdam. It makes Scotland one of the best mapped countries in the world.

1719 The Battle of Glenshiel takes place on 10th June. 1500 Jacobites including some 250 Spaniards are defeated by Hanoverian forces led by Major General Wightman. Contemporary paintings and drawings show Highlanders on the summit of Sgurr na Ciste Duibhe and later their defeated Spanish allies being chased over Sgurr nan Spainteach (*Peak of the Spaniards*). This was the last battle involving foreign troops to take place on Scottish soil.

1746 Charles Edward Stuart and the Jacobite cause are finally defeated at Culloden. The Prince wanders all over the West Highlands before eventually escaping to France. Most of his travels lay to the south of this guidebook area, but he probably spent a night on the summit of Sgurr nan Conbhairean above Strath Cluanie, and then traversed Carn Ghluasaid before descending to a cave in Coire Dho. He also spent two months in the Uists.

Naturalists, Geologists and the Ordnance Survey
1747 William Roy joins a team led by Lieutenant Colonel David Watson and spends eight years producing a map of the Highlands for the military at a scale of 1:21,560. Roy later becomes Major General and it is largely due to him that the Ordnance Survey is set up the year after his death in 1791.

1767 James Robertson, in the course of carrying out a survey of Highland flora, ascends Ben Hope, Ben Klibreck, Ben Wyvis, Scaraben and Morven.

1770s Rev. John Stuart and John Lightfoot ascend many peaks, including Beinn Sgritheall, when botanising throughout the Highlands.

1800s Legend has it that shepherds used to hear a wailing noise above a deep gash (Eag Dhubh na h-Eigheachd) just below the summit of Beinn Alligin, until one of them descends to investigate and falls to his death.

1811–1821 Dr John Macculloch travels extensively while making the first geological map of Scotland single-handed. He writes 'four garrulous volumes on the Highlands and Western Isles'. In the North-West his climbs include Ben Lair, but his finest achievment is undoubtedly his ascent of An Teallach (Sgurr Fiona) – the most significant ascent in the area to date.

1817 William MacGillivray aged 21 ascends An Cliseam '...*in spite of hail and snow, and the furious whirlwinds or eddying blasts that swept the mountain*'. He was a prodigious walker. (At the age of 11 he left Harris to study and travelled on foot from Poolewe to Aberdeen.) A keen but irascible naturalist, he later went on to become Professor of Natural History at Aberdeen University.

1819 Captain Thomas Colby carries out an extraordinary season of mapping for the Ordnance Survey. (His career had nearly been brought to an abrupt halt in 1803, when he lost his left hand following an accident with an exploding pistol. A piece of metal remained lodged in his skull for the rest of his life.) While exploring Inverness-shire, Ross, Caithness and Orkney, with a party of artillery men, and afterwards the western parts of Ross and Skye with a fresh party, Colby traverses on foot an astonishing 1099 miles in 45 days, with only one rest day in the middle. Several summits are visited in the course of this survey work, the most notable in the North-West being Slioch. Colby arranged mountain-top feasts for his men with huge plum puddings at the end of each surveying season. He went on to become the longest serving Director General of the Ordnance Survey (1820–1846), and was responsible for the first detailed mapping of Ireland.

1846 The Inglis brothers – William, Charles and Robert – begin a life-long campaign of peak-bagging throughout the Highlands. Their numerous ascents include Ben More Assynt in 1863.

1850 In the course of settling a boundary dispute a surveyor, George Campbell Smith, places cairns along the march between the estates of Gairloch and Torridon. His route takes him over the ridge of Beinn Eighe.

1851 The first recorded ascent of Beinn Mhor in South Uist is made by Corp. Jenkins of the OS, but trigonometers had been there a decade earlier.

1872 Another boundary dispute sees an employee of Meyrick Bankes place a cairn on Beinn Tarsuinn – one of the remotest Munros.

1876 The summit of the Great Stack of Handa is reached by Donald Macdonald (aged 26) in order to cull sea birds. He crosses hand-over-hand on a rope stretched across the enclosing geo by a team of men from Lewis.

1883 Following a long running dispute over the geology of the North-West, Geikie appoints Peach and Horne to lead a team in mapping the Assynt area for the Geological Survey. One of the survey team, Lionel Hinxman, is a keen mountaineer.

The Climbers Arrive

1888 The Scottish Mountaineering Club is formed.

1890 The second SMC Journal includes two articles on the North-West. Lionel Hinxman describes ascending Canisp with two friends, before climbing Suilven from its eastern end *(A Climb over Suilven)*, and fellow geologist Henry Cadell describes *The Mountain Scenery of the North-West Highlands*.

1891 The fifth SMCJ includes another article by Lionel Hinxman in which he gives an excellent description of *Ben Eighe and the Torridon Hills*. The same year Hinxman makes an ascent of A' Chioch of Beinn Bhan in a thunderstorm.

1892 Charles Pilkington and Horace Walker climb Suilven's Grey Castle by its steep south-western angle. Prof. Ramsay makes a repeat ascent in 1895.

1894 Douglas, Hinxman, Rennie and Macdonald ascend Liathach by the Northern Pinnacles. They then walk through the hills to Strath Carron.

1898 Norman Collie, probably with Cecil Slingsby, makes a part ascent and then full descent of the central buttress of Coire Mhic Fhearchair. He writes that he thinks he has discovered *'the finest rock climb in the British Isles'*.

1899 The first of two successive SMC easter meets is held at Kinlochewe. Lawson, Ling and Glover climb up the eastern end of Liathach and also a gully on Sail Mhor, Beinn Eighe. Inglis Clark, Glover and Gall Inglis climb an impressive face just north-west of a large waterfall on Beinn a' Mhuinidh.

1900 Ling, Mackay, Naismith, Raeburn and Gall Inglis (with an appearance by Munro) make the first winter traverse of Liathach's Northern Pinnacles.

1904 Harold Raeburn and EB Robertson climb a buttress on Sgorr Ruadh.

1906 Dr, Mrs and Miss Inglis Clark and CW Walker ascend the steep western end of Stac Pollaidh (under-graded at Difficult in modern guides).

1907 An audacious attempt on the Barrel Buttress of Quinag by Raeburn, Ling and Mackay only succeeeds after an inspection on a rope from above. Ling and Sang attempt the Nose of Sgurr an Fhidhleir. The fine East Buttress of Coire Mhic Fhearchair is climbed by Gibbs, Backhouse and Mounsey.

1908 A' Chioch of Sgurr a' Chaorachain is climbed by Glover and Ling.

1910 Ling and Glover climb Beinn Airigh Charr (by a more direct line than their foray of the previous year). They also climb on Foinaven and Ben Hope.

1914 Goggs, Arthur and Young climb the 'buttress left of Barrel Buttress'.

1930 M Botterill does some of the first rock climbs in the Outer Hebrides.

1932 Ling writes the *Northern Highlands* guide for the SMC.

1934 Naismith edits the *Islands of Scotland* guide for the SMC.

1951 Frank Cunningham pens a review for the SMCJ in which he describes climbing developments in the Northern Highlands since Ling's guide.

1952 Scott and Mrs Johnstone explore the climbing possibilities in the Outer Hebrides, and make new ascents. (Notes appear in the 1954 SMCJ.)

1955 The Ling Hut is opened in Glen Torridon.

1973 A moratorium is proposed on the reporting of new routes west of the Great Glen (with the exception of Skye) by Ian Rowe and Graham Tiso.

1993 The first comprehensive climbing guide to the Northern Highlands (edited by Geoff Cohen) is published in 2 volumes. The flood gates open...

ENVIRONMENT

With ever larger numbers of walkers and climbers going to the Scottish hills, countryside and coasts, it is important that all who do so recognise their responsibilities to those who live and work in these environments, to our fellow climbers and to the environment in which we find our pleasure and recreation.

The Scottish Mountaineering Club and Scottish Mountaineering Trust, who jointly produce this and other guidebooks, wish to point out that it is in everybody's interests that good relations are maintained between visitors and landowners. The right of access to a climbing, walking or skiing route in any of these publications is based on the individual abiding by responsible Access Codes.

Access

The stag stalking season is from 1st July to 20th October, although many estates don't start at the beginning of the season. Hinds continue to be culled until 15th February. The grouse shooting season is from 12th August until 10th December, although the end of the season is less used. These sporting activities can be important to the economy of Highland estates and it would be a responsible approach to keep disturbance to a minimum during these seasons by following advice from the Mountaineering Council of Scotland (see below) and any reasonable local advice about alternative routes.

It is also important to avoid disturbance to sheep, particularly during the lambing season between March and May. Dogs should not be taken onto the hills at this time, and at all times should be kept under close control. The MCofS and Scottish Natural Heritage also operate a Hillphones service giving daily recorded information of the location of stalking on some estates in the popular hill walking areas.

Climbers and hill walkers are recommended to consult *Heading For The Scottish Hills*, published by the SMT on behalf of the MCofS, which gives the names and addresses of factors and keepers who may be contacted for information regarding access to the hills (see Books, below).

Footpath Erosion

The number of walkers and climbers on the hills is leading to increased, and, in some cases very unsightly, footpath erosion. Part of the revenue from the sale of this and other Scottish Mountaineering Club books is granted by the Scottish Mountaineering Trust as financial assistance towards the repair and maintenance of hill paths in Scotland.

However, it is important for all of us to recognise our responsibility to minimise our erosive effect, so that the enjoyment of future climbers shall not be spoiled by our damage of the landscape.

As a general rule, if a path exists then try to stay on it. If the path is wet and muddy avoid walking along its edges as this only extends the erosion sideways. Do not take short-cuts at the corners of zigzag paths. The worst effects of erosion are likely to be caused during or soon after prolonged wet weather when the ground is soft and waterlogged. At such times a route on stony or rocky hillside is likely to cause less erosion than one on bare soil or grass. Always try to follow a path or track through cultivated land and forests, and avoid causing damage to fences, dykes and gates by climbing over them carelessly.

Bird Life

When scrambling, don't cause direct disturbance to nesting birds, particularly the rarer species, which are often found on crags (eg Golden Eagle, White-Tailed (Sea) Eagle, Peregrine Falcon, Razorbill, Guillemot, Puffin, Fulmar, Kittiwake, Cormorant, Shag, Buzzard, Kestrel and Raven). Usually this is between 1st February and the end of July, but on coasts it may be later; for example, it has been agreed for Handa Island that there will be no climbing from mid March to the end of August. Intentional disturbance of nesting birds is a criminal offence and, if convicted, you face a fine of up to £5,000 and confiscation of climbing equipment. It is the individual's responsibility to find out from the MCofS (see below) about voluntary restrictions at any particular location and to obtain advice as to whether their presence might disturb any nesting birds.

Vegetation

When cleaning routes in summer take care what you remove, some of the flora may be rare. Many crags are designated Sites of Special Scientific Interest (SSSI). This doesn't mean climbing is not allowed, but it may mean there are restrictions on activity. When winter climbing, minimise damage to underlying vegetation by only climbing when it is fully frozen. Crag and Winter Climbing Codes are available from the MCofS (see below).

Litter and Pollution

Do not leave litter of any sort anywhere, take it down from the hill or crag in your rucksack. Do not cause pollution, and bury human waste carefully out of sight far away from any habitation or water supply. Avoid burying rubbish as this may also pollute the environment.

Bicycles

Although the use of bicycles can often be helpful for reaching remote hills and crags, they can cause severe erosion and damage when used 'off road' on soft footpaths and open hillsides. Bicycles should only be used on hard tracks such as vehicular or forest tracks.

Cairns

The proliferation of navigation cairns detracts from the feeling of wildness, and may be confusing rather than helpful as regards route-finding. The indiscriminate building of cairns on the hills is discouraged.

Car Use

Do not drive along private roads without permission and, when parking, avoid blocking access to private roads and land or causing any hazard to other road users.

General Privacy

It is common courtesy to respect personal privacy near people's homes.

Bothies

The Mountain Bothies Association has about 100 buildings on various estates throughout Scotland which it maintains as bothies. The MBA owns none of these buildings, they belong to estates which generously allow their use as open bothies. Bothies are there for use by small groups (less than six) for a few days. If you wish to stay longer permission should be sought from the owners. The increased number of hill users have put a greater strain on the bothies and their surrounding environment. It is therefore more important than ever that the simple voluntary bothy code be adhered to. This and more information can be found on the MBA website <www.mountainbothies.org.uk>:

- If you carry it in, then carry it out and have respect for the bothy, its owners and its users;
- Leave the bothy clean and dry, guard against fire and don't cause vandalism or graffiti;
- Bury human waste carefully out of sight far away from the bothy and the water supply and avoid burying rubbish.

Mountaineering Council of Scotland

The MCofS is the representative body for climbers and walkers in Scotland. One of its primary concerns is the continued free access to the hills and crags. Information about bird restrictions, stalking and general access issues can be obtained from the MCofS. Should any climber or walker encounter problems regarding access they should contact the MCofS, whose current address is: The Old Granary, West Mill Street, Perth PH1 5QP, tel (01738 638 227), fax (01738 442 095), email <info@mountaineering-scotland.org.uk>, website <www.mountaineering-scotland.org.uk>.

SAFETY

Participation

"Climbing and mountaineering are activities with a danger of personal injury or death. Participants in these activities should be aware of and accept these risks and be responsible for their own actions and involvement."
UIAA participation statement

Liabilities

You are responsible for your own actions and should not hold landowners liable for an accident (even if a 'no win, no fee' solicitor tempts you), even if it happens while climbing over a fence or dyke. It is up to you to assess the reliability of bolts, pegs, slings or old nuts on the understanding that they may, over time, become corroded and therefore fail.

Mountain Rescue

In the event of an accident call 999 and ask for Mountain Rescue. This is co-ordinated by the police. If possible give a six figure grid reference, details of the casualty's condition and any help available at the accident site. It is often better to stay with the victim, but in a party of two, one may have to leave to summon help. Leave the casualty warm and comfortable in a sheltered, well-marked place.

Equipment & Planning

Good equipment, clothing, forward planning and navigation skills in the mountains, can all help reduce the chance of an accident. Whether to use a rope for scrambling comes down to personal choice. If there are inexperienced or nervous members in the party then a rope should certainly be carried, and the ability to abseil might well be useful in case of retreat (carrying a sling and a karabiner could well be invaluable). A few routes have a short pitch much harder than the rest of the route (Stac Pollaidh or Corrag Bhuidhe, for instance), and the use of a rope may allow less confident scramblers to complete these.

While mobile phones and GPS can help in communications and locating your position, consider that the former do not work in many places in the north of Scotland and both rely on batteries and electronics which can fail or be easily damaged. Consequently, they can never be a substitute for good navigation, first aid or general mountain skills. In recent years the general carrying of mobile phones has made getting help easier (although there are still many hill areas where there is no coverage). This has unfortunately led to an increase in frivolous calls – in many cases self rescue is both quicker and preferable and an element of self reliance is no bad thing.

Two-thirds of accidents are the result of a lengthy fall, due either to holds breaking or rockfall. About one-third are the result of planning errors – being too ambitious (trying a route that's too hard) or simply failing to judge how long a route will take and becoming benighted.

Maps & Terminology

The Ordnance Survey 1:50,000 scale maps cover the whole area and are the most commonly used. The relevant map is mentioned for each hill. The recently revamped Explorer Series also covers the whole area at 1:25,000 and gives more detail of cliffs, but some sheets are not yet available. The Harveys map is particularly useful for Torridon as it gives detail of ground cover and avoids the need for changing maps on Liathach and Beinn Eighe. Distances and heights in the text are given in metres (abbreviated to m in route descriptions). Left and right are used in the direction of travel (i.e. facing the crag in ascent, facing out in descent). Numbered routes will be found on diagrams close to the relevant text. The numbers of the scrambles and climbs in the text correspond to the numbers on the diagrams.

Symbols are used on SMC maps to indicate different categories of summit. Munro – black triangle (Tops are not marked); Corbett – black circle; Graham – black diamond; Other – crossed circle.

Place names and map references have in general been taken from the OS 1:50,000 Landranger maps. The following maps cover areas in this guide:

OS Landranger Map 9	Cape Wrath
OS Landranger Map 10	Strathnaver
OS Landranger Map 15	Loch Assynt
OS Landranger Map 17	Helmsdale & Strath of Kildonan
OS Landranger Map 19	Gairloch & Ullapool
OS Landranger Map 20	Beinn Dearg & Loch Broom
OS Landranger Map 24	Raasay & Applecross
OS Landranger Map 25	Glen Carron & Glen Affric
OS Landranger Map 26	Inverness & Strath Glass
OS Landranger Map 33	Loch Alsh, Glen Shiel & Loch Hourn
OS Landranger Map 34	Fort Augustus
OS Landranger Map 13	West Lewis & North Harris
OS Landranger Map 14	Tarbert & Loch Seaforth
OS Landranger Map 22	Benbecula & South Uist

Books

The SMC publications *North-West Highlands, The Islands of Scotland including Skye, The Munros, The Corbetts, Scottish Hill and Mountain Names* and *Scottish Hill Tracks* are useful for hill walking routes and general mountain interest in this area. For more information and to order SMC and SMT publications, visit the SMC website <www.smc.org.uk>. See also the list of SMC publications at the end of this guide.

TECHNICAL NOTES

Grades

Scrambling grades are inevitably only approximations, as there is often a great deal of choice of route, so the standard can often be altered to suit differing abilities or conditions. The routes are graded for **dry, summer conditions**, and will become much harder in the wet, especially in the case of the schist or quartzite routes. Very few routes are suitable for descent and in winter they will involve serious winter mountaineering and need the appropriate skills and equipment.

SCRAMBLES

Scrambling covers the intermediate area between walking and rock climbing. The lower boundary is easy to define – once the hands are needed for progress, you are scrambling – but the upper one is more problematic. One approach is to say that scrambling covers rock too easy for most rock climbers to need a rope, another is to say that scrambling becomes rock climbing once the interest of the moves become greater than the interest of the situation.

Grade 1: Easy Scrambles

Experienced hillwalkers will find routes of this grade reasonably straightforward. The moves themselves will not be difficult, and although there may be some exposure, it will only be on easy sections.

Grade 2: Interesting Scrambles

These routes may have awkward moves, sustained scrambling and considerable exposure, but these will not normally occur together. Some routes will have short technically difficult sections, others will be easier but hard to escape from.

Grade 3: Advanced Scrambles

These could have thought-provoking moves in exposed situations or sustained difficult sections. Many scramblers may prefer the reassurance of a rope in places. The route could be hard to escape or retreat from.

ROCK CLIMBS

The rock climbs described in this guide are graded according to the standard adjectival system for summer climbs. Only routes in the two lowest grades are described. (The Easy grade is not recognised here.)

Moderate

Most people will want a rope for outings of this grade. There will be tricky moves in exposed positions and the route could be serious or sustained (but probably not both at the same time). It overlaps with the Grade 3(S) used in some scrambling guides.

Difficult

Technical climbing skills are required here. There could be long exposed sections and hard moves in airy and serious situations. Most will require a rope and retreat could be tricky.

Use of the rope

It should be obvious that a rope will only increase safety if at least one member of the party knows how to use it properly, and if it comes out of the rucksack as soon as anybody needs it. A few slings, nuts and karabiners are also very useful for setting up belays. Should a retreat become necessary a rope can also enable a descent by abseil.

Left and Right

The terms left and right are used when facing the direction being described, i.e. facing a cliff for a route description, facing downhill in descent.

Diagrams

Many of the routes are shown on diagrams close to the relevant text. The route numbers in the text correspond to the route numbers shown on the diagrams.

Recommended Routes

All the routes in this guide are worthwhile. Stars have been awarded based on sustainedness, rock quality, directness of line and the impressiveness of the situations. Only the truly outstanding routes get three stars.

The stars refer to the quality of the scrambling itself, but there are several examples where indifferent scrambling is part of a superb day on the hill – for instance, Suilven or the North-West Ridge of A' Mhaighdean. Because of the distance of this area from centres of population there are some outstanding routes here that few will have heard of. If the Gillaval Dubh or An Groban routes were in Glen Coe, for example, they would be as well-known as Curved Ridge.

First Ascensionists

For many of the outings described in this guide there are no details known about who first ascended them. However, details of the first recorded ascensionists for most of the routes that involve rock climbing are listed in the back of SMC climbing guides to the Hebrides and Northern Highlands. A few are also mentioned in the Mountaineering History section.

AMENITIES

Travel

Trains run up the East Coast as far as Helmsdale and from Inverness across to Kyle of Lochalsh, with useful stations at Achnasheen and Achnashellach. Details of bus and coach services in the Highland Council area can be found on the **Traveline Scotland** website.
<http://80.75.65.35/Highland_Council/timetables_Highland_Council.htm>
These include:

Citylink Coaches (08705 505050) <www.citylink.co.uk/network.htm> (on line booking) run from Inverness to Wick (daily), Inverness to Ullapool (Mon–Sat) and to Kyle of Lochalsh from both Inverness and Glasgow (daily).

Rapsons Coaches (01463 710555) run from Inverness to Ullapool (Mon–Sat).

Tim Dearman Coaches (01349 883585) <www.timdearmancoaches.co.uk>, run from Inverness to Durness via Lochinver (Mon–Sat, Apr–Sept & Sundays in July & Aug).

Westerbus (01445 712255) run from Inverness to Gairloch (Mon–Sat), also Gairloch to Ullapool (Thurs only).

D & E Coaches (01463 222444) also run from Inverness to Gairloch, May–Sept (daily).

Ross's Minibuses (01463 761 250) run a service from Beauly Station to Cannich.

Royal Mail Postbuses run daily from Lairg to Tongue and Kinlochewe to Shieldaig (except Sundays).

Outer Hebrides travel information is given in that chapter.

The infrequency of these services, however, means that most people will arrive by car, most of the roads these days being fast and not generally busy. The **only 24 hour petrol station** north-west of Inverness is at Broadford on Skye, but there are petrol stations at Lairg, Tongue, Durness, Scourie, Lochinver, Ullapool, Contin, Gairloch, Kinlochewe, Achnasheen, Lochcarron, Kyle of Lochalsh, Inverinate and Shiel Bridge. On the Outer Hebrides there are useful petrol stations at Stornoway, Timsgearraidh, Ardhasaig, Tarbert and Leverburgh, all closed on Sundays. Ferry information for the Outer Hebrides is given in that chapter.

Accommodation, shops, tourist information etc.

There are numerous hotels and B&Bs scattered around the area. Most of the former offer bar meals. Booking accommodation ahead is best done through **Visit Scotland** at 0845 2255121 (8am to 8pm) <www.visitscotland.com> rather than through local Tourist Offices – email: info@visitscotland.com.

If you are on the spot there are local Tourist Information Outlets at Strathpeffer (Head Office), Dunbeath, Tongue, Durness, Kinlochbervie,

Ullapool, Gairloch, Achnasheen, Strathcarron, Cluanie Inn and Stornoway (all open all year) and at Bettyhill, Lochinver, Lairg, Beauly, North Kessock, Kyle of Lochalsh and Glenelg (open Easter to October). Most of the small villages have a shop and there are supermarkets in Ullapool, Kyle of Lochalsh and Stornoway. There are small climbing shops in Ullapool (North West Outdoor), Poolewe (Slioch) and Kinlochewe (Moru).

Camp Sites

Dunbeath, Inver Caravan Park, (ND 165 299), 01593 731441.
Talmine, (NC 585 627). Cheap, friendly and a nice beach.
Durness, Sango Sands, (NC 406 679) 01971 511761. Fine clifftop position.
Sheigra, (NC 182 601). No facilities but gorgeous setting.
Scourie, (NC 154 447), 01971 502060. Expensive but restaurant & bar.
Clachtoll, (NC 040 274). Close to beach.
Achmelvich, (NC 054 248), 01571 844393. Superb beach & bouldering.
Achnahaird, (NC 015 137), 01854 612135. Another great beach.
Ardmair, (NH 108 984), 01854 612054. Excellent view.
Ullapool, (NH 125 938), 01854 612 020. Town site handy for pubs etc.
Contin, (NH 457 561), 01997 421351. Quiet site with all facilities.
Badrallach, (NG 065 916), 01854 633281. Quiet scenic spot.
Poolewe, (NG 861 811), 01445 781249. Lochshore site in village.
Gairloch, (NG 797 774), 01445 712 373. Village site, all facilities.
Sands, (NG 759 785), 01445 712152. Expensive but good beach & facilities.
Taagan, (NH 013 637). Basic free site.
Torridon, (NG 905 558). Basic site with nearby bouldering.
Shieldaig, (NG 816 542). Basic village site close to pub.
Applecross, (NG 711 444), 01520 744 268. Peaceful setting with facilities.
Lochcarron, (NG 906 401), 01520 722 245. Small village site.
Cannich, (NH 342 313), 01456 415364. Village site with all facilities.
Shiel Bridge, (NG 938 186), 01599 511221. Friendly site with shop.
Morvich, (NG 961 212), 01599 511354. All facilities.
Uig Sands, (NB 049 329). Basic site by huge beach.
Miabhag, (NG 177 941). Craggy setting.
Horgabost, (NG 047 969). Basic site in stunning scenery.

Climbing Huts

Naismith Hut, (NC 216 118), SMC. On loop road at north end of Elphin.
The Smiddy, Dundonnell, (NH 094 878), JMCS Edinburgh section.
Ling Hut, (NG 957 563), SMC. 300m along path from Coire Dubh car park in Glen Torridon.
Glen Lichd House, (NH 005 173), Edinburgh University MC.

Independent Hostels <www.hostel-scotland.co.uk>

Lazy Crofter, Durness, (NC 402 675), 01971 511202/366. All year.
Kinlochbervie Hotel Bunkhouse, (NC 222 567), 01971 521275. (Awaiting approval 2006).
Kylesku Backpackers, (NC 225 334), 01971 502003. Apr–Oct.
Ullapool Tourist Hostel, (NH 127 940), 01854 613126. All year.
Badrallach Bothy, (NH 065 915), 01854 633281. All year.
Sail Mhor Croft, (NH 064 893), 01854 633224. All year.
Kinlochewe Bunkhouse, (NH 029 619), 01445 760253. All year.
Gerry's Achnashellach Hostel,(NH 038 492), 01520 766232. All year.
Strathconon Inn Hostel, (NH 322 551), 01997 477201. All year.
Cannich Backpackers, (NH 340 314), 01456 415263. All year.
Tigh Isabeal, Camas-luinie (NG 947 283), 01599 588205. All year.
Kintail Lodge Hotel Bunkhouse, (NG 938 197), 01599 511275. All year.
Rockview Bunkhouse, Tarbert, Harris, (NB 155 001), 01859 502211. All year.

SYHA Hostels <www.syha.org.uk>

There is now a central booking number for these – 0870 155 3255.
Helmsdale, (ND 028 155).
Tongue, (NC 586 584).
Durness, (NC 417 672).
Achmelvich, (NC 058 247).
Achininver, (NC 042 056).
Ullapool, (NH 129 940).
Carbisdale Castle, (NH 574 954).
Carn Dearg, (NG 763 776).
Torridon, (NG 904 558).
Glen Affric, (NH 080 202).
Ratagan, (NG 919 199).
Garenin, (NB 190 450).
Rhenigadail, (NB 229 018).
Howmore, (NF 757364).

Weather Forecasts

The one virtual certainty about the weather here is that it will vary over the area of this guide! The Radio Scotland Outdoor Activities Forecast is about the best available – around 7.05pm every evening at present.
Online forecasts are available at:
<www.bbc.co.uk/weather>
<www.metcheck.com/V40/UK/HOBBIES/mountain.asp>
<www.metoffice.gov.uk/weather/europe/uk/nwscotland.html>
<ukie.accuweather.com/adcbin/ukie/ukie_mountain_index.asp>

FOINAVEN & THE FAR NORTH

This area includes everything north of the A838 Lairg to Laxford Bridge road, plus Ben Stack just south of it. In the east the Old Red Sandstone hills of Caithness rise sharply from endless moorland, while in the centre the isolated peaks of Ben Loyal and Ben Hope dominate the north coast. The west is the best, however, where the quartzite crests of Foinaven and Arkle and the prominent spike of Ben Stack look out over miles of contorted gneiss. Foinaven in particular has a concentration of good long scrambles on both gneiss and quartzite.

All these peaks, and the remoter hinterland of the Reay Forest, provide wild rough walking, often with the chance to have a whole mountain to yourself. In places there are long mountain rock climbs, with the 300m high Creag Urbhard on Foinaven taking pride of place. In addition the fringes of the area contain large numbers of short outcrop climbs, on both the sandstone sea cliffs of Caithness and the peerless gneiss of Western Sutherland, with scope for many more in both cases.

MORVEN

706m   OS Landranger 17   (ND 004 285)

This conical sandstone hill is the highest of a compact group in the southern corner of Caithness. On a good day views range from Assynt to the Cairngorms.

1 North-East Ribs   Grade 1
Alt 600m   North-East facing   (ND 006 287)   Map p48

Morven is a steep pull from any direction, but these ribs add some interest to the top part.

Approach
These are most easily approached from Braemore (ND 073 304) following the path to Corrichoich bothy, then continuing directly towards the mountain. Looking up from the north-east three ribs can be seen high up. Go steeply up heather to the left-hand of these.

The Route
Climb the left-hand ridge (the others are similar but with a few harder sections). At the top traverse right to the skyline rib and climb it. There are more similar ribs to the right and the tor to the south of the summit has some boulder problems.

Well worth a visit while in the area is the Smean, the prominent tor between Morven and Scaraben, which turns out to be a complex of rock tors reminiscent of Dartmoor. A keen boulderer could spend hours here.

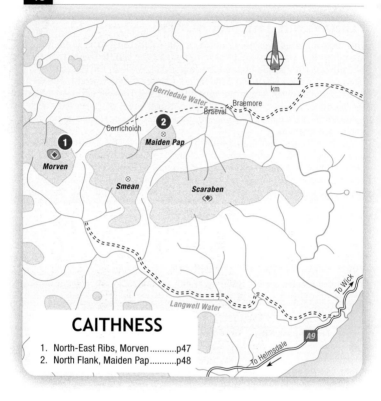

CAITHNESS

MAIDEN PAP

484m   OS Landranger 17   (ND 048 293)

This prominent spike east of Morven is a great little summit.

2 North Flank   Grade 2 or 3   *

Alt 350m   North-East facing   (ND 048 295)   Map p48   Diagram p49
Entertainingly delicate conglomerate slabs.

Approach
From the end of the public road at Braemore (ND 073 304) cross the bridge and take the track running west through Braeval. At the saddle turn left up the wood edge. Continue in the same line up a grassy strip ending about 50m below the crags, then go up left to two slabs at the foot of the face.

MAIDEN PAP

1. North Flank   Grade 2 or 3 *

The Route
The right-hand slab is a delicate Grade 3, the left-hand is Grade 2. Easier slabs and heather follow, then a steeper slab. Now either climb a little prow on the left (Grade 3) or the slab to its right (Grade 2) and go up to an easing. Climb the right edge of the foresummit ahead, starting at a little pinnacle. On the way to the main summit there is a short rib on the left just above the saddle.

On the far side of the summit the north-west rib provides a very short but excellent scramble, steep but on big juggy holds (Grade 3).

BEN LOYAL

764m   OS Landranger 10   (NC 578 488)

This isolated mountain consists of a series of rocky summits linked by grassy saddles, with the northern end dominating the Kyle of Tongue in a large veg-etated cliff. Views range from Orkney in the east along the whole of the north coast to Cape Wrath. The hill is made of an intrusive igneous rock called syenite, similar to granite but with very little quartz. Metamorphic reworking has caused some of the crystals to line up, making it very slippery in places.

3 Sgor Chaonasaid   Grade 2 (and a jump!)   *
Alt 700m   (NC 579 499)   Map p51

The northern peak of Ben Loyal has an impressive north face, unfortunately disappointing from a scrambling point of view, but the spine running south along the ridge is entertaining.

Approach
Walk in from Ribigil south of Tongue (NC 584 547) and follow the track to the cottage at Cunside, with Sgor Chaonasaid towering ahead. A scrappy scramble can be made up the left-hand edge of the north face, starting up isolated slabs at the foot, but a lack of friction on these forces you largely onto steep grass.

The Route
Reaching the actual summit of Sgor Chaonasaid involves an awkward step up. Return the same way, then from the col just south of the summit go up steeply onto the arête running south. Follow this to a scary jump over a gap. This is less than 2 metres, slightly downhill with a good landing, but the penalty for failure is high. Carry on until a steep drop ahead forces a delicate descent right, then make a long step across a gully to a ledge. Go down the arête, then cut back left to a col. Pass the next pinnacle on the right (or detour up it), then pull up steeply at a jammed flake to follow another arête. Where this ends drop down right, then down left easily to an escape. Cross slabs and a rock bridge ahead, then at the end go down right then left to easy ground.

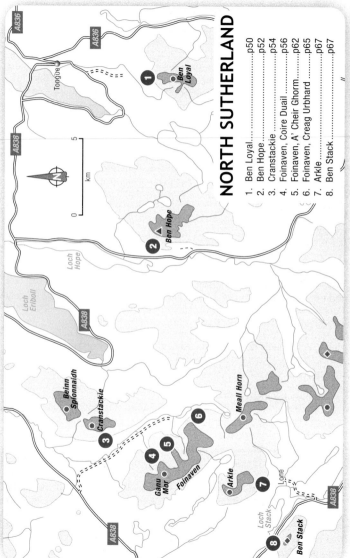

NORTH SUTHERLAND

Ben Loyal — **1**

Ben Hope — **2**

Tongue

Loch Hope

Loch Eriboll

Beinn Spionnaidh

Cranstackie — **3**

Ganu Mor — **4** **5** Foinaven

6

Meall Horn

Arkle — **7**

Loch Stack

Ben Stack — **8**

Lone

N

0 — 5 km

A836

A838

4 Sgor a' Chleirich Ridge   Grade 2
Alt 500m   North facing   (NC 569 492)   Map p51

Nice positions, but not great scrambling.

Approach

Start as for the previous route, then once below Sgor Chaonasaid follow a shelf slanting up right through a beautiful birch wood below the cliffs. Continue along the top of the woods until a steep ascent can be made into the corrie between Sgor a' Bhatain and Sgor a' Chleirich. Go up right to the ridge.

The Route

Avoid the initial slabs, then go up boulders and a groove in an easy angled nose. At steeper rock climb mossy slabs on the left from right to left. Easier ground then leads to a steep clean rib. This is more than scrambling, so go up the gully to the left or the mossy rib left again. Just below the top of the rib traverse delicately left onto the main ridge and go more steeply up this. Finish up either a wide crack (Moderate) or a stepped gully to the left.

BEN HOPE

927m   OS Landranger 9   (NC 477 501)

The northernmost Munro is flanked on its western side by a large and complex cliff with at least six major ridges and numerous minor ones. The two most prominent are at the northern end, separated by a wide gully. Brown's Ridge is the left-hand one, while Bell's Ridge, which is much harder than scrambling, is the right-hand one. Right of Bell's Ridge a grass rake runs up right above a lower steep section to a col on the next major ridge further right (Tower Ridge). Petticoat Ridge runs down into the rake halfway between Bell's Ridge and Tower Ridge.

5 Brown's Ridge   Grade 3   **
Alt 500m   North-West facing   (NC 476 508)   Map p51   Diagram p53

A steep grass approach leads to sustained and exposed scrambling on good holds, then an airy but easy ridge.

Approach

Start at the usual approach to Ben Hope, from the barn at NC 462 477. Go up the path as far as the first shelf, then follow the shelf northwards to Dubh-loch na Beinne. Beyond this two gullies run down the upper cliffs, the right-hand being the start of the rake mentioned above. Start just left of the left-hand gully.

The Route

Go up steep grass left of the first buttress, then more steep grass before cutting through a rock band by a left to right rake. Go up left via a short juggy

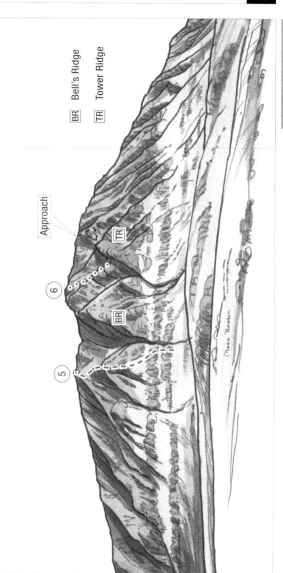

BEN HOPE
North-West Face

5. Brown's Ridge   Grade 3 **
6. Petticoat Ridge   Grade2 or Difficult

BR   Bell's Ridge

TR   Tower Ridge

Approach

wall and more grass to a bigger buttress with overhangs. Left of the overhangs go left up steps and a short wall to more grass. Go left to a grassy bay, then right up this to the skyline and the start of the better scrambling.

Climb a juggy arête and a wide crack, then another steep crack, finishing with an awkward and exposed step right and a hard pull up onto a ledge. Go up just left of the arête, then move right onto it. This is very exposed, but big jugs lead up it to an easing of angle. Follow the arête to the top, easy at first, then with lots of juggy steps and little problems. Where the ridge becomes less defined head up left to clamber up blocks, then more short walls lead to the main north ridge.

A steep nose blocks the way to the main summit. This can be passed at Very Difficult via delicate and exposed ledges on the right. It is much easier to dodge it by way of a gully on the left, returning back right as soon as possible to enjoy the blocky arête beyond.

6 Petticoat Ridge   Grade 2 or Difficult
Alt 800m   West facing   (NC 475 505)   Map p51   Diagram p53

A short juggy ridge, quite exposed, with a purgatorial approach. The latter can be avoided by an intricate and serious descent from the summit.

Approach

The direct way in is to slog up the rake mentioned above, avoiding the steep lower section by traversing in from well to the right. A far more pleasant but serious and exposed alternative is to descend the first major ridge south of Tower Ridge (not the minor ridge dropping from the narrow point of the plateau). Go down about 50m to grass, then slant down right (facing out) on a deer track into the top of a basin. Continue right to a col on Tower Ridge, which is at the top of the rake. Petticoat Ridge starts about 60m down the rake.

The Route

Avoid the first rocks on the right and start either by a slabby rib leading up left to a steepening, dodged by an awkward gully on the right (Difficult), or by coming in by the second grass rake on the right. Either way leads to a vertical tower on the crest. Traverse right below this on small ledges to an easy pull up. Continue up the ridge on huge blocks. Near the top it broadens and steepens, with big holds leading up to the main north ridge above its rock step.

CRANSTACKIE

800m   OS Landranger 9   (NC 350 556)

Although Cranstackie is usually climbed along with its neighbour Beinn Spionnaidh in a short horseshoe from Rhigolter to the west, the mountain's most interesting side is the west flank of the long south ridge. This throws down a row of buttresses offering some good short rock climbs and several

CRANSTACKIE
West Flank

7. Dionard Rib   Grade 3 **

scrambles. In a less isolated setting they would be popular, but here only the most continuous one is described.

7 Dionard Rib Grade 3 **

Alt 250m South-West facing (NC 346 533) Map p51 Diagram p55

Excellent clean gneiss slabs, with a few steeper moves. Quite sustained but not particularly exposed.

Approach

From Gualin House (NC 307 565, parking on the opposite side of the road just to the north) follow the track up Srath Dionard for 5km and ford the river about 100m beyond the first fishermans' hut. If the river is high it will be necessary to contour round the slope from Rhigolter. Above the fording place is a grassy bowl with a steep cliff well above it. To the right are a gully, then broken ground, then a clean rib jutting forward with a steep left-hand face halfway up. This is the route. Right again is a steep reddish cliff, then more ribs, some of which also have good scrambling potential. Steep slopes lead up to the rib, just left of a minor gully.

The Route

The first clean rock starts with an awkward move onto boulders, then follow the right-hand edge to heather. Clean slabs lead to easy ground, then go up heather and small slabs until the rib becomes more definite. Make a hard move onto it, then go up easy slabs to a ledge with a deer path. Another slab leads to a second deer path. Follow the rib on the left in a good position, then go right below a bulge and climb a juggy crack to a heather ledge.

Climb a crack right of centre (hard to start) or an easier crack further right. Now follow the centre of the rib to heather below a steep wall. Dodge this by boulders on the right edge, then go up left to regain the crest. Easy slabs lead to a leaning wall. Pass this by a ramp slanting up right (harder than it looks). An easy rib then leads to a steeper rib up left, started on jugs. A lovely central groove follows, with either a hard and exposed exit on the left or an easier one on the right. Easy slabs run up to broken ground a short way below the ridge.

FOINAVEN

911m OS Landranger 9 (NC 316 507)

One of the finest hills in Scotland, Foinaven consists of a long crest of quartzite with a complex of corries and lateral ridges running off north-east. The main ridge offers some brief easy scrambling at Lord Reay's Seat, but the little-visited Dionard side gives some of the most atmospheric scrambling in the area. The northern routes are mainly slabby gneiss, while further south are quartzite slabs fringing the enormous verticalities of Creag Urbhard.

FOINAVEN - Cnoc Duail

8. Cnoc Duail, North Face   Grade 3 **

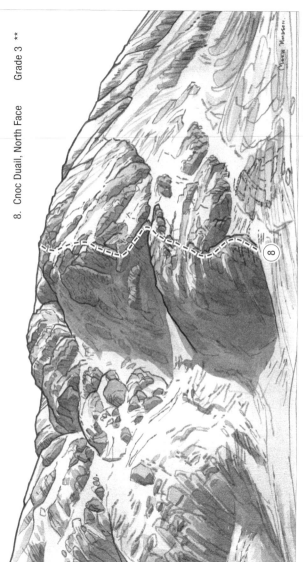

8 Cnoc Duail, North Face   Grade 3   **
Alt 200m, North facing (NC 337 518)   Map p51   Diagram p57

A long slabby route on perfect gneiss.

Approach
From Gualin House (NC 307 565, parking across the road just to the north) follow the track up Srath Dionard to the stream coming out of Coire Duail. Turn right up this until it steepens at slabs. These give a nice prelude, then the main scramble is up left. The left-hand side of the buttress is pinker and steeper. Start at gentle slabs below and right of this, at the left-hand of two main slabby areas.

The Route
Follow walking angle slabs up left, gradually steepening into a more defined rib. At the top move left and climb the next rib, then steeper knobbly rock. Go up to another steepening and climb it (the nose on the right is Difficult). Easy slabs and heather now lead to the base of the upper buttress.

   Avoid the steep wall at the foot on the right (the groove at the right-hand end of the wall is Difficult). Easy steps lead to another steep nose. Go left under this to a long slabby rib, which widens into superb delicate scrambling, sustained and serious. Finish up a well-positioned groove on the right-hand edge. At the top go left and up another short rib. An awkward start leads to a slab and another rib, then short steep walls lead up left to more slabs. The ground now eases off, but more slabby problems can be found on the way to the summit.

 9 Lower Coire Duail Slabs   Grade 3   *
Alt 400m   North-East facing   (NC 323 512)   Map p51   Diagram p59

Enjoyable slabby scrambling but with no real line. Conveniently included between Cnoc Duail and the Ganu Mor Slabs. An easier version slants rightwards to the upper lochan, but the best scrambling leads up left.

Approach
Walk in as for the previous route, then go up Coire Duail to the slabs right of the corrie headwall (or traverse in from Cnoc Duail after doing Route 8). Start at the lowest rock, a steep wall with a slab above, about 20 metres left of a small stream.

The Route
Climb sloping steps at the right-hand end of the wall to reach walking angle slabs and grass. Pass a long red overhang by steeper slabs to its left. When these run out move left to more slabs and a grass terrace. Above this pass a long steep band by steps below a reddish prow, then work up left to grass below a patterned slab. Climb this and slabs above, easing in angle to walking. Climb a steeper red slab on the left, then move right and climb slabby blocks to grass. Broken ground now leads to the summit of Ganu Mor, but more scrambling can be found by traversing off right, slanting up a broken

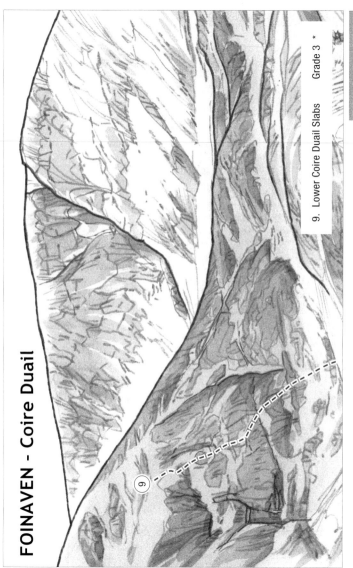

FOINAVEN - Coire Duail

9. Lower Coire Duail Slabs   Grade 3 *

Iain Thow on Lower Coire Duail Slabs (Grade 3), Foinaven
Photo: Noel Williams

FOINAVEN - Upper Coire Duail

10. Ganu Mor Slabs Grade 3 ***

rake, then taking a deer track right until possible to descend to the lochan in Upper Coire Duail.

10 Ganu Mor Slabs   Grade 3   ***
Alt 550m   North facing   (NC 318 513)   Map p51   Diagram p61

A mass of gneiss slabs, quite sustained and serious, but with lots of route choice.

Approach

This forms the south side of Upper Coire Duail above the lochan. Approach either from the previous route as described above, or by slanting up the north flank of Lower Coire Duail to arrive on the right-hand lip of the upper corrie, right of the slabs guarding the entrance. From the lochan walk up the south side of the corrie for 200m to a steep slab on the left with a wide grassy rake running up leftwards from its foot and a pink tongue coming down to boulders on its right. Go 50m up the rake to a moss patch below quartz blotches (a smaller grass rake goes up right from here).

The Route

Climb the slab past the quartz, aiming for a vertical pink dyke. At the base of this take a ledge rightwards onto a big slab. Climb this about 10m right of the pink band, carrying on up the line of a hairline crack. At a grass patch go left and up more slabs, starting at a small left-facing riblet and passing left of a red overlap. The slabs end at a grass terrace with short steep walls above. Take a low angle red ramp left and above its end climb a steep pink dyke. Where this splits take the right branch and carry on up the right-hand arête. Above this boulder problems lead to grass, with the summit of Ganu Mor 150m higher.

11 A' Cheir Ghorm, Twin Caves Ridge   Moderate
Alt 600m   North facing   (NC 330 502)   Map p51   Diagram p63

A' Cheir Ghorm is a narrow quartzite ridge running north-east from the main Foinaven Ridge. It has a 150m high north face broken into a dozen or so ridges. Unfortunately these are very loose, but the situations are impressive. The bottom 30m is steep, then the angle eases. The face is highly confusing, and several of the ridges make reasonable scrambles, the described one being the easiest to identify.

Approach

Approach up Srath Dionard as for the previous routes. Either leave the vehicle track at around NC 353 503 and follow the stream up or cut across from Cnoc Duail after Route 8. At the north-east end of the A' Cheir Ghorm ridge the rock extends the whole height of the face. Near the right-hand edge of this is a deep gully with a scree shoot issuing from it. On either side of this there are small outcrops below the main face. Twin Caves Ridge is the right arête of the gully, with the twin caves at its foot. Start left of these, just inside the gully.

FOINAVEN - A' Cheir Ghorm

11. Twin Caves Ridge   Moderate

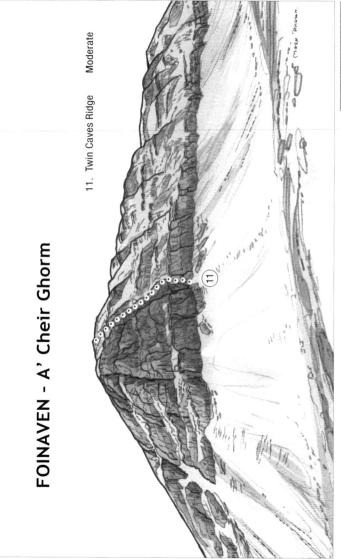

Iain Thow on the left-facing riblet, Ganu Mor Slabs (Grade 3), Foinaven
Photo: Noel Williams

The Route

Go up steeply (loose) and pull up into a minor gully using a jammed block. Climb rightwards onto the arête, where the angle eases and the arête breaks up into short steps. Climb these following the skyline to arrive on the ridge just left of the summit. The A' Cheir Ghorm ridge itself has a narrow section with easy scrambling just before the steep rise onto the main ridge.

12 Creag Urbhard, Upper Slabs   Grade 3   **

Alt 300m   East facing   (NC 353 486)   Map p51   Diagram p66

A large sweep of smooth clean quartzite slabs, sustained and serious. There are no real lines and a vast choice of route. Some areas are quite blank and having been caught out in the middle by a thunderstorm I can vouch for them being desperate in the wet.

Approach

Approach up Srath Dionard as for the previous routes, but continue to the end of the track at Loch Dionard. Follow the pathless west shore of the loch below the main face of Creag Urbhard. Above the south end of the loch is the huge overhanging prow of First Dionard Buttress. Go rightwards up a grassy rake immediately beneath it into the corrie behind Creag Urbhard. On the right the broad South Ridge forms the top edge of the main cliff. This has some easy slabs, but far better is to go further into the corrie to the prominent slabs up on the right, with steeper rock to their left.

The Route

There are so many route options that any line can only be a suggestion. Generally the further right you go the easier it gets (but there are exceptions). Easy-angled broken slabs lead to a bouldery easing at half height. Above this a broken line of overlaps extends across from the steeper rock up left. The best route goes up right to bypass these, then heads back up left to pass under a higher set of overlaps. Once beyond these the angle soon slackens to broken slopes.

13 Second Dionard Buttress   Grade 1

Alt 200m   East facing   (NC 359 485)   Map p51   Diagram p66

Easy slabby scrambling in a wild situation.

Approach

As for Route 12 to the south end of Loch Dionard, then 200 metres further on a wide heathery ramp slants back up right, with broken rock below and a long vertical tier above (Second Buttress). This is not the shattered ramp which starts above the head of the loch and leads into more serious ground. There is a smaller tier above Second Buttress, then a higher tier up and left again contains the Third, Fourth and Fifth Buttresses. Start on the right-hand edge of the heathery ramp, at a thin tongue of slabs.

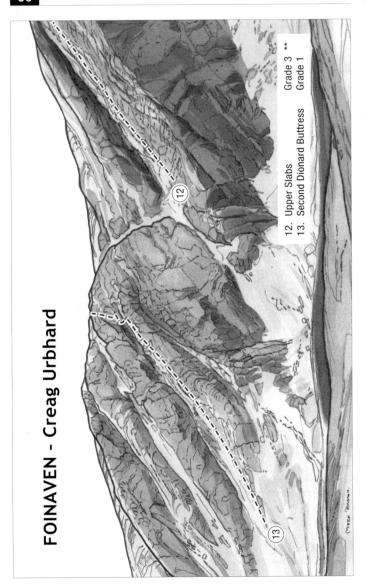

FOINAVEN - Creag Urbhard

12. Upper Slabs   Grade 3 **
13. Second Dionard Buttress   Grade 1

The Route
Go up the walking angle slabs, then up right on heather to the broader slabs which form the top half of the ramp. Go up these, mostly walking but with the odd harder section, to reach a scenic perch on the top of the impressive First Dionard Buttress. A deer track now zigzags up heather on the crest of the buttress, passing a couple of short steep walls. The buttress then broadens, with a few easy outcrops en route.

ARKLE

787m   OS Landranger 9   (NC 302 461)

Another gem of a hill, whose dramatic quartzite ridge curves around a wild corrie. The huge sunny south face offers long though quite broken scrambles, of which the following is the best.

14 South Rib   Grade 2   *
Alt 250m   South facing   (NC 306 441)   Map p51   Diagram p68
A nice line and airy positions, but mostly quite loose.

Approach
From Loch Stack (NC 296 402) follow the track to Lone and just beyond this turn left to reach a small wood below the Allt Horn. Cross bog on the left until steep heather and scree lead up to the first deep cut gully (not the more open stepped groove visible from Lone, which gives a scrappier scramble). The route is the right-hand edge of this, very prominent from a distance.

The Route
Start on the right edge of the gully and climb a crack left of the rib. Climb a steep tower (or an easy rib to its left) to heather, then go up broken rock to a steepening. Climb this direct, then more broken ground. At the next steepening climb an easy stepped slab on the left, with the gully dropping away below. Go up to and climb a groove on the left edge, then shattered ground leads to heather, with the biggest tier ahead. Climb directly up the skyline until an overhang forces you left into grooves. A couple of easy ribs follow before the ground begins to ease off. A slab capped by a striped boulder on the gully edge is worth including before a final tier leads to the shoulder.

BEN STACK

721m   OS Landranger 9   (NC 269 423)

A steep-sided ridge running north-west to south-east, this peak is separated from the rest of this section by the A838 road, but is included here because the easiest access is from this road. The north side has two bands of shaggy cliffs separated by a terrace, with the upper one offering some scrambling.

ARKLE

(14)

Mark Hudson.

14. South Rib   Grade 2 *

Iain Thow on North Flank (Grade 3), Ben Stack
Photo: Noel Williams

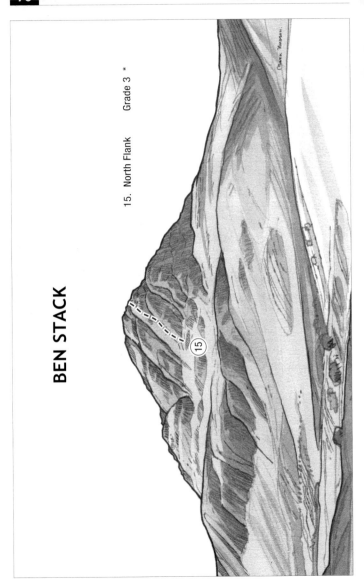

BEN STACK

15. North Flank   Grade 3 *

15 North Flank   Grade 3   *
Alt 450m   North facing   (NC 268 426)   Map p51   Diagram p70

The inward-dipping stratified gneiss gives an easy-angled scramble on small positive holds with good friction and little exposure. Only the early parts are Grade 3.

Approach
Park by the farm building at NC 265 437 and go up the path just west of this to Loch na Seilge. Just before crossing the stream running into the loch turn left up a broken fence. Follow a rough path alongside this until the fence turns right. Leave the path here and traverse up left until below the north face. Ignore the lower broken section and start at a clean slab with a thin blind crack directly above Loch Stack Lodge. This is the skyline seen on the approach and the largest clean mass of rock visible.

The Route
Climb the slab, then another slab above and a hanging rib on the left. Broken ground and more ribs then lead to a roof. Traverse in above this from the left and climb the rib above. Move left to go up an easy rib, then another long easy rib on good rock, then more outcrops until they end. Traverse 20m left to find more rock and string together more ribs until these run out into easy slopes. A few more minor outcrops can be found to reach the ridge west of the summit.

At this point a glance over the other side of the ridge reveals an obvious slabby rib. Traverse across to this and climb it, moving right at the top to finish up another shorter rib.

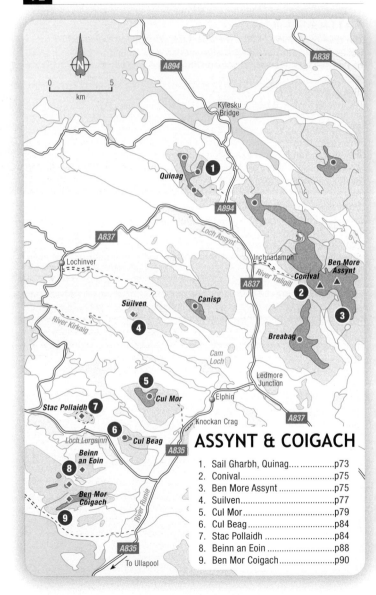

ASSYNT & COIGACH

ASSYNT & COIGACH

The twin peninsulas of Assynt and Coigach are a magical landscape where isolated rocky peaks of Torridonian sandstone dominate a crumpled carpet of Lewisian gneiss. All the main peaks have scrambling about them somewhere, and in Stac Pollaidh and Suilven the area boasts two of the finest and most distinctive peaks in Scotland. Inland, the area is bounded by the more rounded but still rough ridges of Ben More Assynt and its satellites.

QUINAG

808m   OS Landranger 15   (NC 209 292)

A range in itself, this many-topped hill culminates in two huge buttresses overlooking Kylesku. The western face throws down a long line of broken ribs, but the rock is very loose and the faces much steeper than they look from below.

16 Sail Gharbh, East Buttress   Grade 3   *
Alt 300m   North-East facing   (NC 217 300)   Map p72   Diagram p74

Sail Gharbh is the left-hand of the two summits in the classic view from Kylesku. Its left-hand buttress is the least steep, consisting of sandstone tiers on good holds. The route is technically quite hard in places, but without much exposure.

Approach
From the top of the Kylesku to Inchnadamph road (NC 232 274) a good path leads towards Quinag. Where the built stalkers' path ends and the path becomes rougher leave it and contour northwards. Go round below the lowest (wet) tier of Sail Gharbh until this starts to break up. You then reach a grass shelf with rock slabs below and left, and steep ground above.

The Route
Climb a steep clean rib directly above the shelf, then wet steps. Go up left to the next tier, aiming for a clean nose slanting up right. Step onto the nose and go up it into a wet bay. Grovel onto a huge boulder on the right and go up right to easy ground. Walk up right to the skyline and up easy slabby steps to the next and largest tier, which starts with two short stepped buttresses. The next two sections are the hardest, but can be avoided by grass on the right.

Start at a waist-level shelf right of centre and climb direct, then up right, with an awkward step right below a nose. Go up left and just left of the skyline work left up two cracks to a terrace. The easy route comes in here. Climb an obvious central weakness on the next tier, steep at the top. Now climb numerous bands of easy steps until the ground eases to walking. There is a final tier where the buttress runs into the main hill, climbed easily by a gully left of centre.

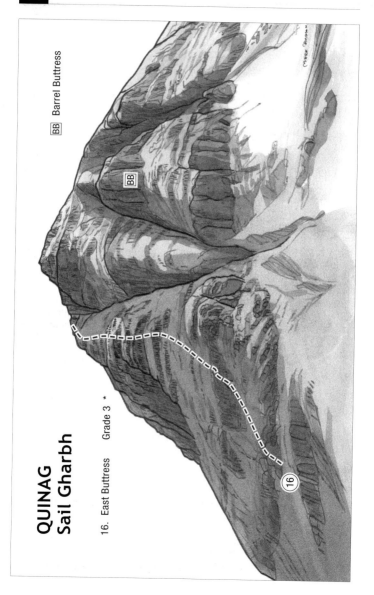

QUINAG
Sail Gharbh

16. East Buttress   Grade 3 *

BB   Barrel Buttress

ASSYNT & COIGACH

CONIVAL

987m OS Landranger 15 (NC 303 199)

This summit and its neighbour, Ben More Assynt, are the culmination of a vast sprawling range separating the distinctive peaks of the west from the rolling moorlands of the east. The south ridges of both hills are narrow and rocky, though not particularly difficult.

17 South Ridge Grade 2 or 3 *
Alt 600m South-East facing (NC 307 191) Map p72

A bit disjointed, but with several enjoyable sections. Quite exposed in places. The initial outcrops are all avoidable, but the upper ridge is not (Grade 2).

Approach
From Inchnadamph take the well-marked path up the River Traligill, forking left along the stream up Gleann Dubh. Where the path goes up left out of the gorge go up right to reach the saddle between Conival and Breabag Tarsuinn. Go through this and take a shelf on the left to two small pools. Slant up bearing right to the lowest rocks on the skyline. Start on the right edge of the right-hand vertical face.

The Route
Climb steeply to a shelf slanting left, which leads to easier ground. Walk up right, linking together small outcrops as desired. As the ridge starts to become better defined climb a steep slab just left of the skyline, then another a little higher, both delicate. Walk up to the towers now visible above.

The first tower is preceded by conglomerate boulders, then climbed on lovely rough slabs to reach more boulders. The second and third towers are climbed easily on the crest, then the ridge becomes mainly walking, although still narrow. A step across a gap is quite exposed, before more broken steps lead to the summit.

A more sustained and steeper start can be found further left, but this is quite loose and has a foul approach up steep scree.

BEN MORE ASSYNT

998m OS Landranger 15 (NC 318 201)

This is the highest peak in Sutherland. It is linked to its western neighbour, Conival, by a shattered quartzite ridge.

18 South Ridge Grade 1
Alt 900m (NC 320 199) Map p72

Mostly narrow but easy, though a couple of awkward bits are quite exposed.

Willie Jeffrey on the quartzite slabs (Grade 2/3) on the west flank of Breabag
Photo: Noel Williams

ASSYNT & COIGACH

Approach
Usually approached via Conival, and done in descent from the summit of Ben More Assynt. However, the scrambling is better south to north.

The Route
Descending from Ben More the first scrambling met is an easy but exposed slab, descended just left of the crest, then a short narrow arête follows. Just before the lowest point a rocky knoll has to be crossed, either directly (delicate start) or on the right (big holds but very exposed). The ascent to the South Top is narrow but easy after a short rock step. Many will return the same way, but a more aesthetic return is to carry on over Carn nan Conbhairean before descending south-west to Dubh Loch Mor, where a grassy shelf leads back to the Conival/Breabag col. Direct descents to Dubh Loch Mor from the ridge are very steep and loose.

Also worth a look if you are in the area are the quartzite slabs on the west flank of Breabag at NC 281 163. These make a fun diversion on the way up the hill (Grade 2/3), and are easily escapable. The prominent slab right of the lowest outcrops is better than the one with a steep left-hand wall further left. Protruding 'pipes' give better friction than usual for quartzite.

SUILVEN

731m   OS Landranger 15   (NC 153 183)

Although a contender for Scotland's finest peak, Suilven has less scrambling than a distant view might lead you to expect. The ridge traverse is a classic for its views and situations, but other routes are either too hard or too vegetated for inclusion.

19 East Ridge   Grade 2 or 3   **
Alt 600m   (NC 157 181)   Map p72

One of the best mountain days in Scotland, but the scrambling is fairly minor. Often very exposed, with superb positions and scenery.

Approach
The saddle between Suilven's two main peaks, Caisteal Liath and Meall Mheadhonach is easily (although steeply) reached from either side, starting either at Inverkirkaig or at a small parking space 1km west of Glencanisp Lodge (NC 107 220), after which the road becomes private. Follow the road past the lodge and take the track up Glen Canisp. After 5km this crosses the river and about 400 metres later a very wet and eroded path goes up right, eventually rising steeply to the saddle. Starting from Inverkirkaig (NC 086 194) a good track leads up past Kirkaig Falls (well worth the short detour) to Fionn Loch. A boggy path heads up from halfway along the loch and another from just before its east end, and these eventually meet and steepen into an eroded route to the saddle.

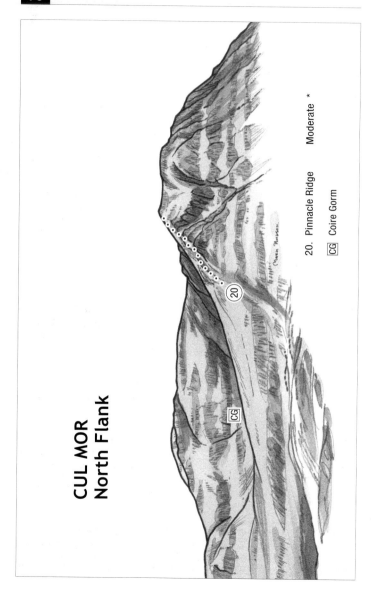

CUL MOR
North Flank

20. Pinnacle Ridge   Moderate *

CG Coire Gorm

The Route

The ascent from the col to the main summit, Caisteal Liath, is easy with the odd rocky step. Return the same way. From the col to Meall Mheadhonach is similar, but with more problems and two unavoidable scrambling sections. Just after the first notch an optional steep wall is Grade 2, then the start of the descent into the second notch is on sloping steps (Grade 1). The other side of the col is another avoidable steep wall (Grade 3). Just before the summit of Meall Mheadhonach is a more sustained section. Start up right to a large block, then go back left to the skyline and up to a hollow tower. From the top of this make an awkward step right and go up to the top.

From Meall Mheadhonach descend a small step and a path zigzags very steeply down to the col below the huge leaning prow of Meall Bheag. Step up and make an awkward move left to a ledge. Follow this further left and climb a groove, then continue left to a terrace below the upper wall. Go up left then right (or direct, slightly harder), then climb a short slab and easy steps to the summit. The descent is easy, with one short narrow section.

In reverse the descent from Meall Bheag can be hard to find. Start well right and zigzag down well-used rock to reach grassy ledges. Follow these left to the saddle.

CUL MOR

849m   OS Landranger 15   (NC 162 119)

The twin peaks of Cul Mor are an easy walk up from the east, but the other sides are steep and rocky, though mostly too broken for quality rock climbing. The distinctive pinnacles on its north-west end provide the best route, but Table Rib is in an impressive setting on the south face.

20 Pinnacle Ridge   Moderate   *
Alt 500m   North facing   (NC 155 129)   Map p72   Diagram p78

Not as good a line as it looks from a distance, but parts of the scrambling are excellent.

Approach

From Knockan Cliff (NC 189 094) take the path leading north. After 2km leave it to traverse rightwards into Coire Gorm on the north side of the summit. Pinnacle Ridge is the right-hand skyline, but once below it the 'ridge' breaks up into several buttresses. The described route starts up the left-hand low one. There are plenty of easier variations, mostly on the left.

The Route

Climb two short steep walls, then the front of a vertical tower by big ledges. The buttress ends after a couple more steps, so cross right and climb the next one past a sharp prow to easy ground. Traverse right under towers to the skyline ridge. Gain this by a slabby ramp on the left and follow the easy flaky ridge. Climb a steeper tower by a grimy chimney (or avoid it on the

Richard Merryfield romping up Pinnacle Ridge (Moderate), Cul Mor
Photo: Noel Williams

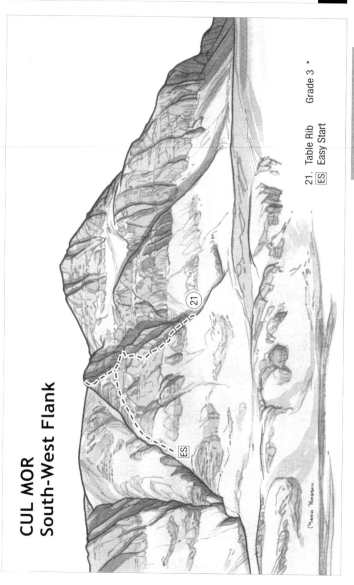

CUL MOR
South-West Flank

21. Table Rib   Grade 3 *
ES   Easy Start

left), then go up cleaner steps. Climb a vertical corner right of a big prow, then bear up right to the next ridge.

This buttress is the crux, avoiding it on the left makes the route Grade 3. Climb a nose by steep flakes, then mossy ledges and a delicate step up lead to the first pinnacle. Hop the gap and descend ahead to a col. Go up the left-hand side of the ridge on excellent clean rock, then up easier ground to say hello to the Old Man (about VS?). Cross the next col and go up broken ground, then up another clean slab on the left-hand side of the ridge. At the next steep section pass the first wall on the left, then a steep slab leads to an easy ridge and the top.

21 Table Rib   Grade 3   *
Alt 500m   South-West facing   (NC 156 114)   Map p72   Diagram p81

A good line and excellent positions, but the actual scrambling isn't as good as it looks from a distance. The start is quite serious, although not too exposed. An alternative start further left avoids this, but it is not as good a line.

Approach
Either walk in from Loch Lurgainn (NC 126 089) via Loch an Doire Dhuibh and scramble up the Allt Lochan Dearg (avoid the two main falls on the right) or traverse west from the usual path to Cul Mor from Knockan Cliff (NC 189 094) to go down past the dramatically situated Lochan Dearg a' Chuil Mhoir. Take a shelf north-west from here, then slant up to the face. Table Rib is the left-hand rib on the main steep face, before the cliffs break down into open slopes. Start in the steep gully to its right.

The easier start (Grade 2) is reached by carrying on along the shelf below the cliffs until the third gully comes down. Go up the near edge of this, mostly on a zigzag deer path. Once above the steep cliffs go up right to join Table Rib at a grassy col.

The Route
Go up the gully and its left-hand branch to slimy slabs with a columnar vertical cliff up to the right. Start left of the centre of the slabs and work up left until it is possible to traverse left to reach the skyline at a block. Climb the crack behind this to a larger block. Bridge up behind it, then climb a crack left of a steep nose. An easy ridge now leads to a saddle at the top of the initial slabs.

Broken ground with occasional problems leads to a steep wall crossing the ridge. Climb this by a grassy gully on the right, gained by a rounded groove right again. The ridge now opens out and the easier version comes in from the left. Climb stepped prows ahead to a pinnacle and a larger nose. Grovel onto a boulder left of the overhang and go up, then more easy steps lead to a level ridge. The sting in the tail is a hard little overhang (avoidable), emerging on the Table.

CUL BEAG
West Flank

22. Lurgainn Edge   Grade 3 ***

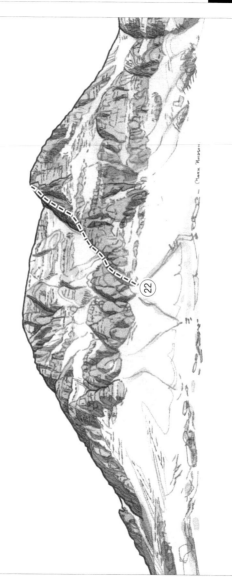

22

CUL BEAG

769m   OS Landranger 15   (NC 140 088)

Like its bigger namesake, this is another isolated hill with steep faces on the north and west. The north face is steep and damp, but the west face contains one superb scramble, with more possible.

22 Lurgainn Edge   Grade 3   ***
Alt 500m   West facing   (NC 138 088)   Map p72   Diagram p83

An outstanding route, traditionally graded Difficult but really more of a scramble. Superb situations make up for a purgatorially steep approach.

Approach

Park by Loch Lurgainn just east of Linneraineach (NC 126 089) and start up the path to Loch an Doire Dhuibh. At the top of the trees leave this and head up direct across pathless moorland and steep heather, aiming for the right-hand side of the prominent central Y-shaped gully. Go up steeply to the first rocks on the right-hand side of the gully.

The Route

Climb three short stepped outcrops, then go up into a minor gully, where a path develops. Follow this up to more rock and an open scoop. Go up the left-hand arête of this (loose at the top), then up right below a jutting nose. Go up left to broken ground, then up right to cleaner rock. A vegetated groove left of this leads to the top of the tier. Things now improve.

From the lowest point of the next tier climb flake cracks to heather. Carry on up easier rocks, climbing little ribs on big rounded holds. A steeper wide flake crack is interesting (easier to the left). When the ridge narrows climb a steep tower with a thin crack, then keep on direct up the crest to easy ground and a narrow neck. Either climb the overhang direct (Difficult, but only one move) or dodge it by a gully to the left. The next rounded overhang is harder, but easily avoided by an exposed ramp on the right, then cutting back left to the top. A short walk leads to the summit.

STAC POLLAIDH

613m   OS Landranger 15   (NC 107 106)

An amazing mini-mountain, little more than 600m high, but as craggy and spectacular as you could wish. Its pinnacled summit ridge provides excellent scrambling at a variety of grades, with many possible variations. The new path round the back is infinitely better than the old eroded slog.

23 East-West Traverse
Alt 500m   (NC 110 105)   Map p72

An easy and a harder line are described, but variations are legion. The true

*Paula Hamilton-Gibson on the crux (Difficult) at the West End of Stac Pollaidh
Photo: Iain Thow*

summit lies at the westernmost end of the ridge. This is guarded by an unavoidable small tower, which involves a couple of moves of about Difficult. Many parties are content to visit a cairned summit a little to the east of the true summit. The direct route to the true summit from the west is given Difficult in climbing guides, but is severely undergraded.

Approach
From the car park at Loch Lurgainn (NC 107 095) take the good track uphill, bearing right at the fork to go round the east end of the hill. For the second two options continue around the northern flank and then ascend to a saddle on the summit ridge.

The Routes
a) East End   Grade 2 or 3   *
At around the 400m contour bear up left to minor rocks. Follow these rather scrappily to the eastern summit. Descend to a notch, then climb awkward grooves on rounded steps to another top (Grade 2). An easy descent leads to the main saddle. If reaching the eastern summit from the saddle the descent into the notch feels very insecure and is at least Grade 3.

b) West End   Grade 3 or Difficult   ***
From the saddle pass left of the first steep wall. Go a short distance up the first gully and climb the right-hand of two corners in its left wall, with an obvious flake crack at the top (Difficult, exposed). This corner can be avoided by going up the next gully along to reach the ridge, making the route Grade 3 (to the cairned summit). Follow the ridge along to the next pinnacle, dodge this on the right and go up a gully to regain the ridge. Follow this to a short drop with an airy step across. Go up a short steep problem and along to a short delicate descent (easy gullies either side). From the notch go up slabs and the ridge becomes easy, with minor problems if desired, until it flattens out. Keep right of boulders on the crest to a short awkward sidle along an overhung ledge above a gully. Climb slabs beyond and follow the ridge left-wards to the cairned summit. The best return route from this summit is by the Grade 1 route described below.

  Access to the highest top is blocked by a short vertical tower (Difficult). This can either be climbed steeply on the right, traversed on the left with a hard start or squirmed around by a groove below and left. Up by the steep way and return by the squirm is probably the easiest combination. The summit is close beyond.

c) West End Easy Route   Grade 1   **
From the saddle pass left of the first wall, the first steep gully and two more open ones. Regain the ridge either via the third open gully, with a steep move at a short jammed boulder (awkward but not exposed), or by the next wide gully along (easy but loose). At the notch above the jammed boulder go right to reach easy ground and follow this up, crossing a transverse barrier to

Noel Williams on the South-West Flank of Sgorr Deas (Grade 3), Beinn an Eoin
Photo: Iain Thow

where the ridge flattens. Keep right of boulders on the crest to a short awkward sidle along an overhung ledge above a gully. Climb slabs beyond and follow the ridge leftwards to the cairned summit. Access to the highest top is blocked by a short vertical tower (Difficult). Return the same way.

BEINN AN EOIN

618m   OS Landranger 15   (NC 105 064)

This twin peaked hill is often thought of as part of Ben Mor Coigach, but is actually separated from it by a 300m gulf. The saddle between them is dominated by the huge prow of Sgurr an Fhidhleir with its classic HVS rock climb up the Nose, but the blunter rib opposite provides good though disjointed scrambling, and the ridge between the two summits also has its moments.

24 Sgorr Deas, South-West Flank   Grade 3   **

Alt 300m   South-West facing   (NC 100 062)   Map p72   Diagram p89

Problems on small outcrops to start, with a superb sustained finish.

Approach

From the east end of Loch Lurgainn (NC 138 067) a boggy path leads southwest up the Allt Claonaidh. Where this reaches the deer fence go right and follow the fence around the north side of Lochan Tuath. Just beyond the col of An Clu-nead the path descends slightly and you start to see along the west face of Sgorr Deas. Start on the small slabby buttresses on the right, at a triangular slab with a steep start.

The Route

Swing left onto the slab (hard but avoidable) and climb it, continuing up several short walls on good holds, bearing slightly left to an easing of angle. Two more short walls can be taken in before the ground flattens out.

Above is a deep gully on the left, with steep grass right of it and steep outcrops right again. Work a way up these latter, easier than they look, to reach a steep rock band running across from the gully on the left. Climb the right-hand end of this on good holds, then bear left up more grass to reach the nearest outcrops.

Climb a small corner, then a flake right of a larger one, escaping left at the top. Go up a series of slabby flakes on big rounded holds, very sustained but with a wide choice of route. As the rib becomes more defined the flakes lead into a groove just right of the skyline. Climb this, then a short steep crack. After one minor outcrop the ground eases, with the summit not far away.

25 Sgorr Tuath, South-West Ridge   Grade 2

Alt 500m   South facing   (NC 105 073)   Map p72

A series of short problems, avoidable and not exposed, give a pleasant way of climbing the ridge.

BEINN AN EOIN
Sgorr Deas

24. South-West Flank   Grade 3 **

Beinn an Eoin viewed from Sgurr an Fhidhleir, Ben Mor Coigach
Photo: Iain Thow

Approach
Almost invariably approached over Sgorr Deas.

The Route
From the Deas/Tuath col go up to a wall on the left and climb its left arête on big holds. Carry on up more outcrops on the ridge line to reach a steep wall at the top. The best line is left of centre, just left of the steepest section. Climb a groove leftwards to finish on the arête.

BEN MOR COIGACH

743m OS Landranger 15 (NC 094 042)

A complex of peaks rather than the simple ridge that is usually first seen, the west ridge is narrow but easy, with the west end of the south face providing the scrambling.

26 West Ridge Direct Grade 3 **
Alt 550m West facing (NC 082 034) Map p72 Diagram p91
A minor diversion from the path, short but on sound rock in good positions, high above the sea.

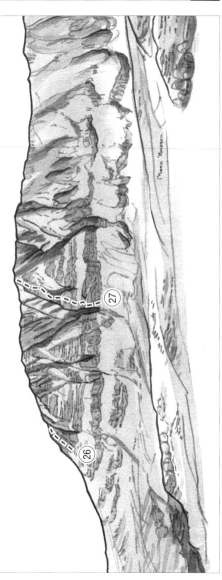

ASSYNT & COIGACH

BEN MOR COIGACH
South Face

26. West Ridge Direct Grade 3 **
27. Isle Martin Buttress Grade 2/3

Approach
Park at Culnacraig (NC 064 041 – take care not to block the turning space) and go up the path just right of the bridge. At the first shoulder traverse right and cross the Allt nan Coisiche just above the waterfall. Go up right to a shelf to see three buttresses on the end of the ridge, just right of the path. The left-hand one is a broken Grade 1, the central has a vertical finish, the right-hand one is the route described. A few easy rock steps lead up to it.

The Route
Start with a short crack, then a wide steep crack above (or an easy groove to the right). Another crack/groove follows, finishing just left of a prow. From a niche on the right go up the crack above for a few metres, then step left and climb the left arête, with one delicate step halfway up. An easy angled ridge now leads to a steepening, climbed by another delicate slab (homesick grit-stone climbers will enjoy the jamming crack on the right). Go left up easy ground into a bay and climb the tower on the left. A few short steps lead to the ridge, where some added excitement can be contrived by following the crest (path on left).

27 Isle Martin Buttress   Grade 2/3
Alt 400m   South facing   (NC 087 033)   Map p72   Diagram p91

This is the second major buttress along the south face. It is technically quite easy, but serious, with a messy start leading to better things above.

Approach
Follow the approach for the previous route to the shelf, then continue right to follow a good sheep track along below the main South Face. Pass over a lower buttress and cross a gully, then a few metres beyond is a left-slanting heathery groove. Start here.

The Route
Climb the groove, avoiding the steepest bit on the left to emerge on the left skyline above the main gully. Zigzag up heather to boulders perched on the left arête below a steeper face. Traverse right past a leaning block and bear up right on more open heather. All this is very exposed. Climb a right-slanting slabby groove, finishing on the right to reach a terrace. Go up left to a small undercut slab below a larger tier. Climb the slab from the right, then traverse left below steeper rock to a short groove. Climb this, then bear right up better rock to reach a shoulder and easier ground. Go up the ridge ahead, including problems as desired. Near the top the ridge is split by a minor gully. The right-hand branch has better rock, with a steep finish up juggy flakes, while the left-hand branch requires a devious route around leftwards to start. Where the ridges rejoin a steep chimney in the tower ahead is a Difficult variation, or go round to the right. A few easy steps with optional problems lead to the summit ridge.

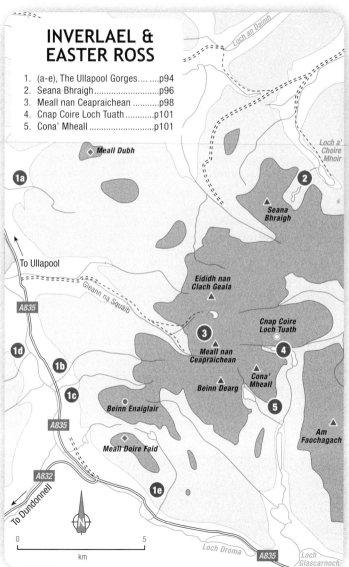

INVERLAEL & EASTER ROSS

Loch an Daimh

Loch a' Choire Mhoir

Meall Dubh

1a

2

Seana Bhraigh

To Ullapool

A835

Gleann na Squaib

Eididh nan Clach Geala

Cnap Coire Loch Tuath

3

4

1d

1b

Meall nan Ceapraichean

Cona' Mheall

1c

Beinn Dearg

5

Beinn Enaiglair

A835

Am Faochagach

Meall Doire Faid

A832

1e

To Dundonnell

N

0   5
km

Loch Droma

A835

Loch Glascarnoch

INVERLAEL & EASTER ROSS

This is the vast sprawling range north of the Ullapool road, culminating in Beinn Dearg and Cona' Mheall. Most of the area is an extensive upland plateau, rimmed to the west by a semicircle of higher summits and cut by deep craggy-sided valleys. The rock is mainly schist, often vegetated, but in places it runs to some long buttresses and clean slabs. Cona' Mheall and Seana Bhraigh provide the best routes. In addition to the areas described, the south flank of Carn Alladale (NC 410 895) is a pleasant easy scramble up huge boulders, while the area around Glenbeg Bothy (NC 314 835) has a scatter of mainly slabby crags, but the scrambling is scrappy relative to the effort involved in reaching it. The Alladale Slabs (NC 375 872) give a choice of steep blank quartzite or equally steep heather, while the long flank of Beinn Dearg above Gleann na Sguaib is mostly too steep for scrambling, although an excellent winter climbing venue.

THE ULLAPOOL GORGES

OS Landranger 20

Around the head of Loch Broom are a number of gorges, of which the spectacular Corrieshalloch Gorge is the best known. In dry weather this can be waded up as far as the falls. Just to the west is the equally impressive Cuileig Gorge, but the central section of this involves swimming. Several steeper gorges come down the hillside into the lower glen.

 ### 28a Ardcharnich Gorge   Grade 2
Alt 50m   West facing   (NH 174 885)   Map p93

The lower gorge is easy but very overgrown, while the upper gorge is extremely impressive, but blocked by impassable falls. It also has very loose walls and is difficult to swim out of while wearing boots and a rucksack! The right branch starting at the mouth of the upper gorge is quite long and pleasant.

 ### 28b Allt a' Bhraighe   Grade 1
Alt 150m   South-West facing   (NH 198 816)   Map p93

A deep gorge of no great difficulty, but it would be hard after heavy rain. Two impassable falls are easily avoided.

Approach
Park opposite the Wood Turning Centre at NH 195 811 and follow the path up from the left-hand side of the car park entrance. Cross a wider track and slant up leftwards to a sharp bend, where a steep muddy pathlet slants down into the gorge.

The Route
A few small pitches lead to an impassable fall avoided by steep scree on the

left. The shelf across to the top of the fall is very loose, so go over the top of the spur to rejoin the stream. More level stream bed follows, then the final fall is avoided by grass on the left.

28c Allt na h-Ighine   Grade 1

Alt 200m   West facing   (NH 200 813)   Map p93

Another easy but scenic gorge, unfortunately with an impossible finish.

Approach

Follow the previous approach as far as the sharp bend, but continue right-wards up the path to a bridge.

The Route

Descend into the stream on the left and pass the stream gate. Lots of boulder hopping with fallen trees and the odd minor pitch follows. Crossing a conglomerate boulder on the right by a little fall is the best bit. A larger fall appears on the left, climbable at Grade 3, as is the next small fall above, but the next (hidden) fall is not, and the escape here is loose and exposed, so best to go up the open gully on the right just before the large fall.

28d Allt a' Gharbhain   Grade 2

Alt 50m   North-East facing   (NH 182 824)   Map p93

Probably the best of the bunch, deep-cut and narrow, with more sustained scrambling than its neighbours.

Approach

From the crossroads north of Inverbroom Lodge follow the minor road and track to the ruins of Garvan. Go through the gate between the ruin and the barn to its left, then 20 metres up take a sheep track left through gorse to the stream.

The Route

The stream is easy at first, with one awkward step on the left at a smooth slab. The first large fall is started wetly on the right and finished up a stepped rib in the centre (quite exposed). Go right into a small gorge, climbing another fall on the left, then crossing right just below the top. An obviously impassable fall comes in from the left and it is best to escape right here up steep vegetation. The upper gorge can be reached by a steep loose slimy gully on the right and an exposed grass traverse, but the small falls above are not worth the nervous energy expended in reaching them.

28e Allt Leacachain   Grade 2

Alt 300m   South facing   (NH 233 764)   Map p93

A more open stream scramble, with all difficulties avoidable if desired.

Approach

From parking at NH 235 760 follow the track north-west alongside the pipeline to the small dam.

The Route
The stream largely consists of easy slabs, with the odd steeper step. The highlight is a short shuffle along horizontal cracks on the left, followed by a long step across the stream onto the lip of an overhang.

SEANA BHRAIGH

927m   OS Landranger 20   (NH 281 878)

One of the most remote Munros, Seana Bhraigh is rimmed by large vegetated cliffs which provide superb winter routes. The spike of An Sgurr projects northwards from the plateau and is one of the few mainland summits only reachable by scrambling.

29 An Sgurr Ridge   Grade 1 or 2   *
Alt 450m   North facing   (NH 298 887)   Map p93   Diagram p97
A blunt ridge with schist outcrops leading to a sharp peak in a remote situation.

Approach
A long way from any direction! Loch a' Choire Mhoir is reached by a private vehicle track up Strath Mulzie, where a mountain bike would be extremely useful. Alternatively another private road leads up Glen Achall to Loch an Daimh. From there fork right to take a stalkers' path up alongside Allt nan Caorach and across a saddle to reach Loch a' Choire Mhoir. From the foot of the loch cross the stream and head up south-west into the mouth of Luchd Choire.

The Route
A small outcrop above the moraine at the corrie mouth is Grade 2, easily avoided. Where the steep wall on the left finishes go left onto the ridge and climb it on blocky rock (Grade 2 direct, easier on the right). Carry on up the skyline, zigzagging up two steeper vegetated sections to reach a level shoulder. Short outcrops lead to a pink slab, climbed on the arête, then more broken ground leads to walking as the ridge narrows.

Keep to the bouldery crest until a steeper prow forces a move right (loose). Carry on up the crest to another steepening. A path zigzags up this (or Grade 2 direct). The angle now eases and short steps lead to the top. Descend via an exposed path just left of the crest (not obvious to start). From the saddle two short easy steps lead to a grassy ridge and the plateau.

30 Corriemulzie Rib   Grade 3 or Difficult   **
Alt 600m   West facing   (NH 295 882)   Map p93   Diagram p97
A spiky rib, quite steep at first, with an exposed crux just below half height.

Approach
As for the An Sgurr Ridge as far as Luchd Choire, then continue to the

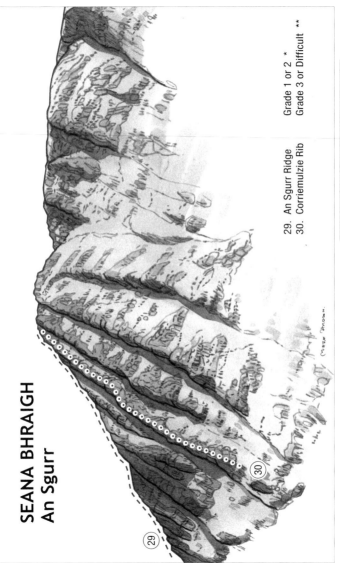

SEANA BHRAIGH
An Sgurr

29. An Sgurr Ridge — Grade 1 or 2 *
30. Corriemulzie Rib — Grade 3 or Difficult **

lochan. The face consists of six ribs, of which the left-hand two are short and the right-hand one is grassy. The described route is the left-hand of the remaining three, which starts lowest on the face, directly above the outflow of the lochan. Go up broken ground to the first steep rock, starting by a rock table.

The Route
Climb slabs to a ledge, then go up the right-hand edge of a V-shaped recess, steep and juggy. Climb a steep crack, then a slab above, starting at a quartzy block. Vegetated slabs and broken ground lead up left to more sustained rock. After a short slab climb a groove with an awkward start to break through steeper rock. Now climb tiers of slabs on the crest, some quite steep but all with good holds, to reach a huge perched block.

The clean slabs above are the crux. Start with a flake crack trending right, then when it bends left either go straight up and over an airy bulge on good holds (Difficult) or bear up right to climb an easier crack above the gully. Both ways lead to a mossy ledge with easier slabs above. Go up these and blocks to a saddle halfway up the ridge. A well-defined ridge of easier mossier rocks leads to the main ridge just north of the summit of An Sgurr. Reach the plateau as for Route 29.

MEALL NAN CEAPRAICHEAN

977m   OS Landranger 20   (NH 257 825)

A grassy plateau with a rocky west face, this is often linked with Beinn Dearg to give a fine day out. Good stalkers' paths make the access easy.

31 West Face   Grade 2
Alt 750m   West facing   (NH 256 832)   Map p93   Diagram p99
Small buttresses lead up to a schist slab prominent from the approach up Gleann na Sguaib.

Approach
Take the forest track from Inverlael up into Gleann na Squaib and fork left at NH 234 835. Just before reaching Lochan a' Chnapaich leave the path and bear right to the lowest point of the screes. Go up right to broken outcrops, the lowest on the slope.

The Route
Climb the outcrops, then move right to a wavy slab. Climb this left to right on sharp quartz holds. Start the next rib on the right and go up the nose to grass. A rock band now crosses the slope, climbed by a prominent quartz band. Bear up right to a ridge on the skyline. An awkward start leads to grass, then a steeper cracked nose leads to delicate slabs. Follow these to the top.

MEALL NAN CEAPRAICHEAN

31. West Face   Grade 2

CNAP COIRE LOCH TUATH

32. South Face   Grade 3

CNAP COIRE LOCH TUATH

884m OS Landranger 20 (NH 282 827)

This minor summit at the end of Meall nan Ceapraichean's east ridge has a 300m south face with large patches of slab.

32 South Face Grade 3
Alt 600m South facing (NH 283 824) Map p93 Diagram p100

A slabby wander up a large face. Quite intimidating, but a lot easier than it looks and with plenty of route options. Best avoided in the wet.

Approach

Loch Tuath at the foot of the face can be reached by following the path up Gleann na Squaib from the head of Loch Broom and descending eastwards from the saddle at its top. A shorter but rougher approach is to walk in up Coire Lair, starting as for the South Ridge of Cona' Mheall (Route 33), and then continuing up past Loch Prille (scrambling right of the falls) to reach Loch Tuath. Cross the stream at the outflow of the small lochan just below Loch Tuath and go up to the lowest outcrop – a scrappy slab.

The Route

Climb the slab, then a cleaner slabby nose. Dodge a vertical wall on the right and go up left to the large area of slabs in the centre of the face. Climb the right-hand edge of these, passing just right of a prominent dark overlap. When the slabs steepen escape right to grass (this is possible at several levels). Go up the grass then traverse left to boulders above the slabs. Climb a grooved rib with squarish overlaps to grass and boulders. Up right is a clean rib with a steep juggy start. Climb this then a choice of minor outcrops to the top.

CONA' MHEALL

980m OS Landranger 20 (NH 274 816)

Beinn Dearg's smaller and more graceful partner has a rocky ridge running north-west to south-east, with buttresses falling 300m into Coire Ghrannda.

33 South Ridge Grade 1 *
Alt 650m South facing (NH 275 804) Map p93

Easy slabby outcrops lead up to a narrow ridge. A great way up the hill, but with only minor scrambling.

Approach

From the A835 just west of Loch Glascarnoch take an initially inconspicuous path starting 400m east of Loch Droma, which leads to the Allt a' Gharbhrain. Go up this until it can be conveniently crossed, then go up the opposite slope to Loch nan Eilean. Continue past this on a shelf leading into the mouth of Coire Ghrannda. Above the outflow from the loch is a broad slope with numerous slabby outcrops.

The Route

Link together outcrops (generally Grade 1 but harder moves can be found) until the buttress coalesces at a scree fan. A path now runs up directly ahead, but the ribs to the right are worth including. Join the main ridge and follow it up. This is mainly narrow and grassy but with a short steep descent to a col and a couple of rock steps beyond. After two minor tops the ridge broadens and runs up to the main summit.

34 Twisted Rib Moderate *

Alt 600m South-West facing (NH 269 809) Map p93 Diagram p103

There are huge amounts of feasible scrambling on this face, the buttresses generally getting harder northwards. Twisted Rib is fairly central, directly above the head of the loch. Steep outcrops with lots of route choice lead to a better-defined slabby buttress, exposed at the top and tricky in the wet.

Approach

As for the previous route to Loch a' Choire Ghrannda, then follow the east side of the loch to crags above the north end. Start at the third buttress from the right, with a long low overhang at its foot.

The Route

From just right of the overhang climb slabs up left to a nose. This is steep, so go a long way left to a ramp leading up left to pass the main cliff. Go right and slant right up slabs, then more slabs and small outcrops lead to a big terrace.

Climb the right-hand side of a vertically grooved nose, then go up to the next tier, easily climbed by a rib on the left. On the next crag step right from boulders onto a nose and go up. The next band is steeper. Climb a square groove, with a hard move left at the top to a ledge. Go up detached blocks at the left-hand end of this, then easy slabs. Go left and up a broad shattered rib, which becomes the left edge of the buttress. Carry on up this to the top. The last section involves an exposed move up right on large flakes just left of the arête.

From below the last steep section it is possible to traverse right across the gully onto the next buttress and climb its slabby arête. This is sustained Moderate, but less exposed.

35 North-East Slab Moderate **

Alt 650m North-East facing (NH 280 820) Map p93 Diagram p104

A single 120m slab of schist, easy-angled but with some fairly blank sections and one awkward overlap. A confident scrambler on a dry day will find it mostly walking with one tricky step, but for the nervous it will be gripping, and in the wet it is lethal.

A serious and committing route in a remote situation.

CONA' MHEALL
South-West Face

34. Twisted Rib   Moderate *

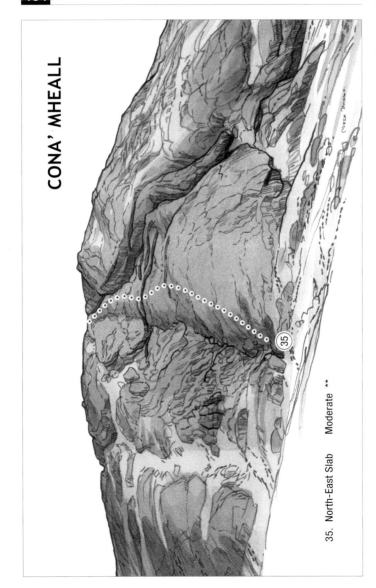

CONA' MHEALL

35. North-East Slab   Moderate **

Approach
The slab is high above the south side of Loch Tuath, which is reached as for Route 32.

The Route
Start up the right-hand side of the central groove and go up until a short curving overlap completely crosses the slab. Climb this left of centre, only one move, but hard enough to make the exposure of the sweep of slabs below very noticeable. Carry on up the narrowing recessed slab, funnelled between the steeper areas either side, with a few delicate sections before it runs out into the hillside. Minor changes in angle drastically alter the difficulty, but the main thing is to avoid wet areas. There are a couple of minor rock steps at the top of the east ridge.

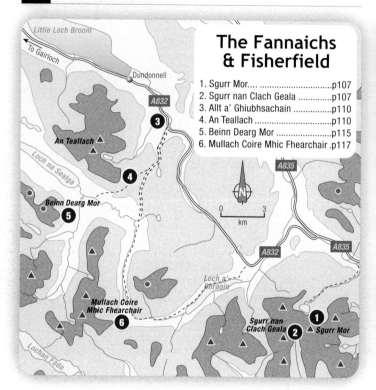

FANNAICHS & FISHERFIELD

The Fisherfield Forest, sometimes called the Great Wilderness, comprises a horseshoe of predominantly sandstone peaks around Gleann na Muice. The scrambles here involve long days and feel quite remote. The western fringes of the area are best approached from Poolewe and are described in the next chapter, while this chapter deals with those routes usually approached from the north. The dominant peak of the area is the mighty An Teallach, a range in itself. The traverse of its pinnacled main ridge over Corrag Buidhe is one of the best days out the Scottish hills can offer. Although this is closer to the road, it is still a big day and should not be underestimated. Further east lie the Fannaichs, predominantly grassy hills with wild open corries. Here a few buttresses offer scrambling approaches to the main ridges, adding interest to a day spent linking the summits.

THE FANNAICHS

OS Landranger 20

These broad sweeping ridges make for good easy walking linking a number of Munros, while the little-visited corries below provide a few scrambles.

36 Sgurr Mor, North Spur   Grade 2
Alt 850m   North-East facing   (NH 205 722)   Map p106

A succession of outcrops coalesce into a sharp ridge leading to the area's highest summit. This looks impressive from a distance, but is very mossy and broken on close acquaintance. All difficulties are avoidable if desired.

Approach
From the west end of Loch Droma (NH 254 755) take the vehicle track up to and along Allt a' Mhadaidh. A smaller path continues to Loch a' Mhadaidh. Go up left on grass to the foot of the North Spur, which is quite broad at the bottom. Start at the lowest clean rib on the left-hand side.

The Route
Go up the juggy rib to a big boulder, then continue directly up moss and boulders to the left-hand side of steeper rock above. Climb mossy slabs with big quartz crystals, then a steeper buttress with big flakes to arrive on a blunt ridge. Mossy outcrops with a few optional harder problems lead to a grassy platform. Above this the ridge narrows but eases and steep airy walking leads to the summit.

37 Sgurr nan Clach Geala, Slanting Buttress   Grade 3 **
Alt 700m   East facing   (NH 191 718)   Map p106   Diagram p109

Steep tiers climbed on big positive holds in a superb situation. The two biggest tiers are both easier than they look and can be avoided on the right.

Approach
Best approached from the north by crossing the saddle of Am Biachdaich, starting from either Loch a' Bhraoin or Loch an Droma. From the saddle traverse down south-east below the cliffs. Slanting Buttress is the inclined buttress starting below and right of the main buttresses. Start at the bottom left-hand corner, at the mouth of Slanting Gully, which bounds the main cliff on the right.

The Route
Go up right onto the buttress and up easy steps. As the gully on the left narrows go up crinkly slabs on its edge (awkward) or avoid them on the right. Reach a large sloping grassy shelf below a steep tier. Climb brown slabs near the left-hand end, then go up to an overhang on positive holds. Go up right below the overhang and back above it on a ledge, then up to another terrace. Climb the first clean rib from the left, which is steep but juggy. At the large overhang traverse airily right and go up the next rib. On the next tier

FANNAICHS & FISHERFIELD

Marco de Man on Slanting Buttress (Grade 3), Sgurr nan Clach Geala, Fannaichs
Photo: Iain Thow

SGURR NAN CLACH GEALA

37. Slanting Buttress   Grade 3 **

(37)

climb the left-hand rib and go up to another terrace, with the buttress now opening out. Climb an easy rib ahead and another up left to more ledges. Go up left to another juggy buttress and the top.

AN TEALLACH

1062m OS Landranger 19   (NH 068 843)

A massive mountain with many summits, An Teallach would be many people's choice as the best hill in Scotland. The pinnacled main ridge is a superb scramble, hard or easy according to choice. There are also a few nearby routes, but fewer than you would expect from the amount of rock, as the massive horizontal bedding of Torridonian sandstone mitigates against good vertical lines.

38 Allt a' Ghiubhsachain   Grade 2
Alt 50m   East facing   (NH 110 857)   Map p106

The slabs in the lower part of this stream can be used either as a roadside evening scramble or combined with the next route as an approach to An Teallach. Low water conditions are essential.

Approach
From the road follow the true right (south) bank of the stream through rhododendron jungle to enter the stream at easy slabs just below a ruined hut on the far bank.

The Route
Go up the slabs and follow the left-hand side of the stream round below steep clifflets. Just above the hut cross the stream and go up to a small gorge, where an escape up the right wall is necessary. Regain the stream as soon as possible and use a rib in the centre, then the left wall to boulders. Cross to the right bank and exit up a steep corner above a large pool, a little way back from the fall. Above the falls follow shelves on the left wall, then round a corner and go up left of a larger fall, escaping left at the top. The falls above are discontinuous (and sometimes impossible), so cross back over and join the path.

39 Ghiubhsachain Slabs   Grade 3   *
Alt 250m   North-West facing   (NH 100 842)   Map p106   Diagram p111

Short but fun slabs covered with incut quartzite holds.

Approach
From the top of the previous scramble continue up the path into Coir' a' Ghiubhsachain. Quartzite cliffs line the east side of the valley, and the described route is at the far end of the initial section, roughly opposite the corrie of A' Ghlas Thuill and 100 metres or so before a wide break in the cliffs. They are the lowest slabs on the right-hand end of this lower scarp.

AN TEALLACH
Coir' a' Ghiubhsachain

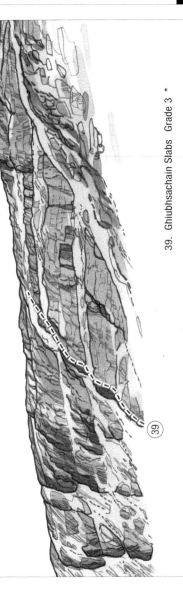

39. Ghiubhsachain Slabs   Grade 3   *

Noel Williams on the lower section of the Corrag Bhuidhe Traverse (Moderate)
Photo: Iain Thow

The Route
A short steep tier leads to a ledge, then climb open smooth slabs with delicate incut holds. A second steeper tier is climbed direct up a ladder of larger incuts.

40 Corrag Bhuidhe Traverse Moderate ***
Alt 950m (NH 065 832) Map p106

One of the best ridges in Scotland. A hard start leads to exposed scrambling over airy pinnacles. Best tackled south-east to north-west as the harder bits are then climbed up not down, but if going the other way beware of descending the end of the ridge directly. This is steep, exposed, often slippery and has been the scene of numerous accidents. Cut down right well before this.

Approach
From the Corrie Hallie car park (NH 114 850) follow the path up Gleann Chaorachain, forking right onto the path to Shenavall, then leaving it after about 1.5km to climb up right over Sail Liath. Follow the ridge along over Stob Cadha Gobhlach and up to the top of the South Buttress of Corrag Bhuidhe. This latter section is Grade 2 if all the outcrops are taken direct (there is a path on the left). From the top of the buttress follow the ridge along and up, with some very easy scrambling. A small pinnacle marks the start of the serious stuff, with the Bad Step prominent above.

The Route
The Bad Step can be tackled direct, but this is steep, greasy and exposed (Difficult). Better is to take a path running left below the cliff to reach a steep clean slab with a flake crack on its left. The lower branch of the path bypasses all difficulties (and all the fun?). Climb the crack (awkward to start), moving right onto the slab as soon as possible to go up left onto a shoulder. Climb a short corner on the left and follow polished steps up left to grass and the ridge. Follow this left to a col.

From here all difficulties can be easily bypassed by a path on the left. More interesting is to go up the next top just right of the arete and follow the skyline. Descend either via an easy gully on the left or by the delicate and wildly exposed end. Pass two minor pinnacles and climb the ridge up ahead over tottering blocks, then a narrow level arête leads to another steep exposed descent at the far end. The next top has an awkward rounded start and leads to the summit of Corrag Bhuidhe. After an easy descent simple scrambling takes you over the airy perch of Lord Berkeley's Seat and on to Sgurr Fiona. A superb circuit is to carry on over Bidein a' Ghlas Thuill and take the ridge running south-east. At the saddle before Glas Mheall Liath cut off right and descend steep grass to Loch Toll an Lochain and a classic view. From the north-east corner of the corrie a small path leads down into Coir' a' Ghiubhsachain and the road (very wet in the rhododendron jungle at the end).

Noel Williams ascending the flake crack, Corrag Bhuidhe Traverse (Moderate)
Photo: Iain Thow

41 Sgurr Ruadh   Grade 1

1/DEC 2020 20 MM

Alt 550m   North facing   (NH 040 854)   Map p106

Easy steps add interest to an unusual way up An Teallach.

Approach

Follow the path up the east side of Ardessie Falls from NH 054 896 and a rougher path along the Allt Airdeasaidh. Cross the mouth of Coire Mor to the foot of the ridge, at the left-hand side of which are a few bouldery outcrops, starting at a bent fence post.

The Route

Climb the bouldery outcrops, then a few small faces to reach the ridge proper. Go up a flaky rib, then the next outcrop either by the easy gully in the centre or the ribs on either side. More ribs follow, then a little boulder problem on the skyline leads to an easy narrow ridge and the first top. There is another minor outcrop on the way to the main top of Sgurr Ruadh, and a few more can be found further along the ridge, which has stunning views out over Loch na Sealga. *START AT SKYLINE, GULLY HAS BELAYS LEFT, LEFT RIB HAS GEAR + TURF.*

BEINN DEARG MOR

910m   OS Landranger 19   (NH 032 799)

Not being a Munro, this splendid peak gets somewhat neglected, being best known as the backdrop to the usual view of Shenavall bothy. Although mostly quite vegetated, it provides a couple of good ridge scrambles, the South-East pinnacles and the rather steeper East Buttress.

42 East Buttress   Grade 3   **

Alt 350m   North-East facing   (NH 044 801)   Map p106   Diagram p116

Sustained scrambling on clean rock, mostly Grade 2 but with a couple of harder sections. Quite steep and occasionally exposed, but also very juggy.

Approach

From the road at Corrie Hallie (NH 114 850) take the track south-west up Gleann Chaorachain, then fork right to reach Shenavall bothy (the route can be shortened by 7km by using the bothy for an overnight stay). Cross the river and take the rough path south-west to another river crossing at Larachantivore. In wet weather both these crossings can be tricky, sometimes impossible. Slant rightwards up rough heather and boulders to the foot of the buttress.

The Route

The lower part of the buttress is poorly defined. Pick a way around several steep walls, mostly on heather but with some blocky scrambling. As the outcrops start to coalesce into a ridge a steep thin pillar of blocks provides a good introduction. Climb the next tier centrally on big boulders, starting with an awkward mantelshelf. A short tier above turns out to be a detached

BEINN DEARG MOR

42. East Buttress   Grade 3 **
43. South-East Ridge   Grade 1/2 *

boulder, quitted on the right. Go left and clamber up what can only be described as gigantic scree. Tackle the more sustained rock above by flakes in the second niche from the left, then climb the wide crack above, finishing on the right arête. Go up the left arête of the next tier, then the slab above, then move left and do the same again. All these difficulties are avoidable on the left.

The arête gradually becomes heathery, with easy pinnacles. Climb a steeper prow on its right arête to boulders, then descend steeply, easiest on the left. Above the col take a very exposed grass ledge out right to blocks on the arête, then ascend easy slabs and go up right to the crest. From the lowest point of the next tier follow slabs up right to a steeper tier. The chimney ahead is squalid, so go left and up a grassy ramp to easy ground. Ledges lead back right to the crest, which leads to the south peak.

43 South-East Ridge   Grade 1/2   *
Alt 700m   South-East facing   (NH 034 791)   Map p106   Diagram p116

A narrow ridge with some easy pinnacles, generally Grade 1, but with a couple of sections that deserve Grade 2 if at all wet. The approach is quite steep and rough.

Approach

As for the previous route to Larachantivore, then slant up south-west. A band of vertical cliffs blocks direct access into Beinn Dearg Mor's south-east corrie, so go up steeply before reaching this, then traverse left into the corrie. A strange rock crevasse runs across the mouth of the corrie, crossable at either its right-hand end or its highest point. Go up left to the start of the ridge.

The Route

At first the crest is rocky but easy, up short steps and over two minor towers. When it bends right and becomes narrow stay on the crest until just before the first pinnacle, then cut down left through a cleft into a gap between the pinnacle and slabs beyond. Go through the gap and up a shallow groove on the right (care needed in the wet). Cross a broad pinnacle and descend just left of the far end, then another short drop leads to a col. Walk up to another pinnacle, descending first on the left, then on the crest. The last step down to the col is steep and slippery. There are several more short steps on the ridge before it merges into the broad summit slopes.

MULLACH COIRE MHIC FHEARCHAIR

1018m   OS Landranger 19   (NH 052 735)

The highest point of the main Fisherfield horseshoe, this rocky peak throws out a long ridge eastwards into the remote country at the head of Loch a' Bhraoin, giving a grand expedition.

MULLACH COIRE MHIC FHEARCHAIR

44. East Ridge   Grade 2 **

44 East Ridge   Grade 2   **

Alt 350m   East facing (NH 077 728)   Map p106   Diagram p118

Really two scrambles in one, the first being steep rough gabbro slabs, not sustained but with some tricky moves, generally avoidable, while the second is a sharp ridge with shattered pinnacles, easy but quite exposed.

Approach

From the road at NH 162 761 take the track to Loch a' Bhraoin, then follow the path along the north shore and up the valley until it turns northwards towards Loch an Nid. The East Ridge is directly ahead, starting as a steep broad spur (Tom an Fhiodha). On the right-hand side of this are vegetated vertical cliffs, while the left-hand side has more broken outcrops. Halfway along is a pink slab at the foot, just above the end of a broken wall. Start about 50 metres left of this at a narrow buttress between two short gullies.

The Route

Either start up the left-hand side of the buttress (hard), or traverse in from the right. Carry on up easier slabs until the two gullies converge. Go into the right-hand one briefly, then up slabs on the left to the top of the buttress. Follow broken slabs and heather above, passing left of a larger cliff. Once above this go right across the gully and up knobbly outcrops until the easy ground to the left finishes. Go left and up steep rough slabs, then climb two easy outcrops. Go up left again and climb a steep pink slab, then further left to a steeper buttress. Start this by a thin pink rib on the right-hand edge, then move left and up an exposed ramp. Easier outcrops now lead to the top of Tom an Fhiodha.

Walk up over Sgurr Dubh to a narrow arête, then descend a shattered ridge. The pinnacles can be crossed or dodged on the left. Go up a blunt tower and the ridge swings right airily. Follow it down to an overhang, avoided on the left. The final pinnacle can be crossed or avoided on the left before a sharp arête leads to easy ground. A pleasant narrow ridge continues over a minor top to the summit.

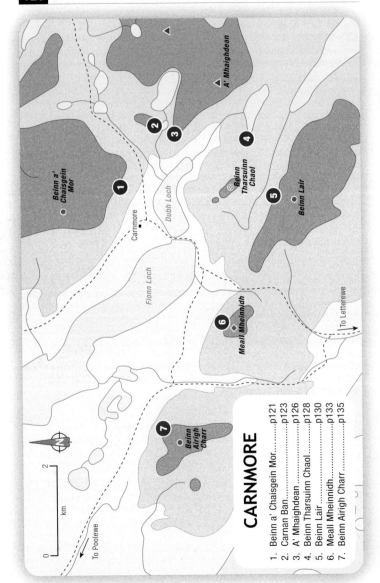

CARNMORE

A' Mhaighdean

Beinn a'
Chaisgein
Mor

Dubh Loch

Beinn
Tharsuinn
Chaol

Beinn Lair

Carnmore

Fionn Loch

Meall Mheinnidh

To Letterewe

Beinn
Airigh
Charr

To Poolewe

km

CARNMORE

Carnmore is a scrambler's heaven, with several lifetimes' worth of rock. A ring of rocky peaks surrounds the basin of the Fionn Loch, those on the north-east side being largely gneiss and those on the south-west being horn-blende schist. The gneiss provides mainly slabby routes on perfect clean rock, while the schist gives more broken routes of over 300 metres on largely inward-dipping holds. Most of these routes are too far from the road to do comfortably in a day, and with so many excellent routes close together it is far better to plan a trip with at least a couple of overnight stays. The barn at Carnmore is open and free (outside the stalking season), while there are many excellent camping spots nearby. On the approach from Poolewe there are a number of notices forbidding camping, but these are not enforced outside the stalking season.

From Poolewe (parking NG 858 808) follow the private road southwards, forking left on the estate road to Kernsary. Go up past the keeper's cottage and half a kilometre beyond this turn right into the wood. Keep on the forest track beyond the turning marked on the map and turn right onto a newer path to a stile (NG 908 788). A good path leads past Loch an Doire Crionaich and crosses the stream at the mouth of Srathan Buidhe (more directly than the map shows). This continues to cross the causeway between Fionn and Dubh Lochs and reach Carnmore Lodge, with the barn a few 100m to its left.

BEINN A' CHAISGEIN MOR

856m   OS Landranger 19   (NG 982 785)

An unimpressive hill from a distance, but on the south side are the rocky tor of Sgurr na Laocainn and the superb Carnmore Crag, home to some of the finest mountain rock climbs in Scotland. The two scrambles described use the flanks of these on immaculate gneiss.

45 Grey Ridge   Grade 3   **
Alt 300m   South-West facing   (NG 982 773)   Map p120   Diagram p122

Originally described as a Moderate rock climb, this gives excellent slabby scrambling with the odd steeper move.

Approach

From Carnmore Lodge go up beside the stream between Carnmore Crag and Sgurr na Laocainn. On the right edge of Carnmore Crag is a narrow gully, Grey Ridge being the broad rib right again. Start at a quartzy rib in the centre.

The Route

Go up the rib, then up right to climb a steeper slab by an ill-defined juggy crack. More slabs lead to a vertical wall. Start at the right-hand end of the

BEINN A' CHAISGEIN MOR

45. Grey Ridge   Grade 3 **
46. Sgurr na Laocainn Right-Hand   Moderate *

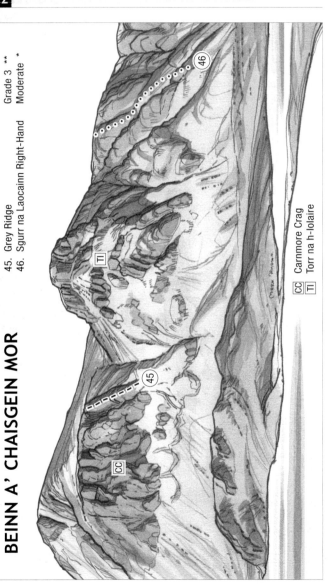

CC   Carnmore Crag
T   Torr na h-Iolaire

overhang or at a steeper crack just left, then follow the crack up superb slabs, steepening slightly at the top. Move left to the skyline and climb easy ribs to open ground. Above are a few boulder problems, notably a steep pinnacle (Difficult), with a step (or fall!) across to the main cliff.

46 Sgurr na Laocainn Right-Hand   Moderate   *
Alt 350m   South-West facing   (NG 988 768)   Map p120   Diagram p122

Sustained and committing, on good rock but with some vegetation. The finish is good but disjointed.

Approach
From Carnmore Lodge take the path up rightwards below Sgurr na Laocainn (Torr na h-Iolaire). Right of the main face is a small pale face low down, then right again is a grassy gully, then another small face. Right of this are two prominent gullies, the right-hand very deep at the top. The route climbs the buttress between these, starting on the left edge of the left-hand Gully, at a small rib.

The Route
Climb the left edge of the rib, which is steep but positive, then move right and go up a vegetated rib, quite steep at the top. A little higher cross the gully on the right to the bottom of the main buttress. Go up the centre of this until it steepens, then move left and up a ramp. Traverse back up right with a vertical wall above. Break through this by a chimney, which is hard to enter (crux). At its top step right and go up slabs to vegetation. Easier slabs lead to heather, bypassing an overhang on the left. Then follow more slabs on the left edge, with good cracks at steeper sections, until a final bulge is passed by an airy step right onto the lip of the overhang.

The buttress now peters out, so cross the gully on the left and either follow easy slabs on its far edge or go up left to more sustained rocks in the centre of the buttress. Go up these on contorted juggy rock, with much variation possible. Finish up shattered boulders.

CARNAN BAN

650m   OS Landranger 19   (NG 999 764)

A minor summit overshadowed by its famous neighbours, but with excellent scrambling on perfect gneiss, verging on easy rock climbing in places.

47 Pocket Slab   Moderate   *
Alt 500m   North-West facing   (NG 997 763)   Map p120

Steep slabs with nice moves but not much of a line. Often wet, but worthwhile in the dry for the amazing contorted rock.

Approach
From Carnmore Lodge take the Shenavall path up eastwards for 1.5km. At

the top of the zigzags cross the stream on the right above its gorge and head south-east towards Fuar Loch Beag. Where the stream from this emerges from the boulders below it head left. High up and facing west is the large mass of Barndance Slabs, with a steep base and an overhang at the bottom right. Pocket Slab is right of these and faces north-west, with two grass rakes slanting up left and pocketed rock above.

The Route
Follow the lower rake up, then where it ends carry on in the same line on juggy pocketed rock to reach a long grass ledge below an overhang. Go up from the left end of this on even bigger pockets until eventually an overhang forces you rightwards to the top of the crag. There are many easy slabby craglets above on the way to the top of the hill.

48 Cakewalk   Difficult   **
Alt 550m   South-West facing   (NH 001 762)   Map p120   Diagram p125
Mostly pleasant slabby cracks, exposed in places, but with a short steep crux.

Approach
As for Pocket Slab to the outflow from Fuar Loch Beag, then follow the northern shore to the 100m high Maiden Buttress above its north-east corner. This contains several excellent Severes, while Cakewalk climbs the far right-hand edge. Start just before an open gully (descent), below a narrow reddish slab which starts at about the same level as the big overhang.

The Route
Climb cracks just right of a small overlap, then the slab above until the cliff steepens. Follow a gangway on the right, then pass large detached blocks and climb a thin crack to a shelf. On the left is a steeper thin crack, quite hard but only for a couple of moves. This leads to a platform from which easy but nicely positioned slabs continue slanting rightwards up the edge of the buttress to the top.

49 Doddle   Grade 2   *
Alt 550m   South-West facing   (NH 002 762)   Map p120   Diagram p125
A slabby rib of perfect gneiss, neither exposed nor serious.

Approach
As for the previous route. This is the separate rib just right of the descent gully on the right-hand side of Maiden Buttress.

The Route
Start up easy angled slabs below and right of the start of Cakewalk. Transfer to steeper slabs on the right and go up centrally, pulling through a small overlap at a crack. Go up to another steepening and pass this on the left arête. Finish direct on excellent slabs.

CARNAN BAN

| 48. | Cakewalk | Difficult | ** |
| 49. | Doddle | Grade 2 | * |

A' MHAIGHDEAN

967m   OS Landranger 19   (NH 007 749)

Probably the remotest Munro, A' Mhaighdean throws down a long stepped ridge to the north-west, with cliffs on both flanks. The ridge itself has a couple of short easy scrambling sections, but more serious routes can be found on the huge west face.

 50 North-West Ridge   Grade 1 or 2   *
Alt 550m   North-West facing   (NG 997 761)   Map p120

A superb way up the hill, but only minor scrambling.

Approach

From Carnmore Lodge follow the approach as for Route 47 as far as the outlet of Fuar Loch Beag.

The Route

Go up rightwards onto the ridge, with optional easy slabs. As the ridge narrows go up slabs below a prominent perched block. Above this go up a left slanting slab below a nose. The ridge now broadens, although still with easy slabs possible. Where it steepens either go up a slab direct at Grade 2 or avoid it on the right. The rock now changes to sandstone, and at the next saddle an open gully descending right from a perched block marks the approach to Red Slab (Route 51).

Two short steps are easily climbed centrally, then walk to another steepening and go up steps in this. As the ridge narrows, cross a neck, then a few metres later cut down left, then go right through a notch. Pass right of a small pinnacle and then a much larger one to reach broken ground and the top. The pinnacle can be traversed at a loose and exposed Difficult by climbing a steep groove in the left-hand arête, then descending the east arête and a vertical corner just right.

 51 Red Slab   Difficult   ***
Alt 750m   South-West facing   (NH 002 754)   Map p120   Diagram p127

A sustained and wildly exposed route on amazing rock – a solid conglomerate consisting entirely of holds.

Approach

Although the route can be approached from below it is far better to access it from the North-West Ridge of A' Mhaighdean (Route 50). Follow Route 50 as far as the top of the open gully just after the start of the sandstone. Descend the gully and follow the bottom of the cliff leftwards (looking out). Pass underneath the first buttress (Conglomerate Arête, Very Difficult), then cross the next gully, going up slightly. Continue under the first part of the next buttress to reach the Red Slab, which has a very undercut right arête.

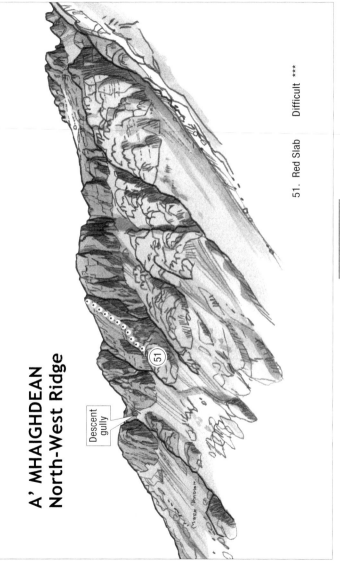

**A' MHAIGHDEAN
North-West Ridge**

Descent gully

51

51. Red Slab   Difficult ***

CARNMORE

The Route
Start as far right as feasible and go up bearing right to a small ledge. Traverse right on this to the edge, then go up to a terrace with huge blocks above. Go diagonally right to a block on the skyline. Climb the arête in a stunning position on small but positive holds to reach a terrace below the top. Climb onto a block and up a final steep wall on good holds.

52 Kids' Ridge Grade 3 or Difficult **

Alt 500m South-West facing (NH 005 743) Map p120 Diagram p129

A succession of outcrops leads to good clean slabs with steeper sections, quite intimidating from below. Much variation possible.

Approach
From Carnmore Lodge go down to the causeway and turn left to follow a rough path along the south shore of the Dubh Loch. Carry on up the valley to Gorm Loch Mor. 200 metres east of the outflow from the loch a deep gully comes down with a steep red right-hand wall. Left of this is a black niche down which a stream sometimes dribbles. Start at a rib down left from this, at the top of a boulder field.

The Route
Climb vegetated slabs to grass, then more slabs to a clamber over boulders. Pass right of a large red boulder, then climb blocky slabs above it. At a vertical wall go left until it gets less steep, then climb it past a large pocket. Go up grass to a clean outcrop, gained from the left. Go up the crest to boulders. Above these go right onto a red rib (starting this direct is Difficult). Go up the rib and grass above, then climb a steep awkward red wall to reach more sustained rock.

Follow slabs up to a steepening (Difficult direct), then take a ramp right and climb a steep corner. More slabs lead to a steeper red nose. Climb the left edge of this, then go up pocketed slabs and a corner. Work up right to the crest, with steeper clean slabs off to the left (these can be taken direct at Difficult). Climb the crest and a juggy groove above, then a steeper nose by rightward-running cracks. The angle now eases, so go up left and follow the slabby crest, passing a superb pocketed slab, until the rock peters out just before reaching the main ridge.

BEINN THARSUINN CHAOL

652m OS Landranger 19 (NG 989 744)

An intermediate ridge between A' Mhaighdean and Beinn Lair, this well hidden hill is very craggy, particularly on its north side. The prominent Ghost Slabs above the Dubh Loch are impressive, and provide some scrambling up behind their right-hand edge, but the steeper buttress above the west end of the Gorm Loch Mor is better.

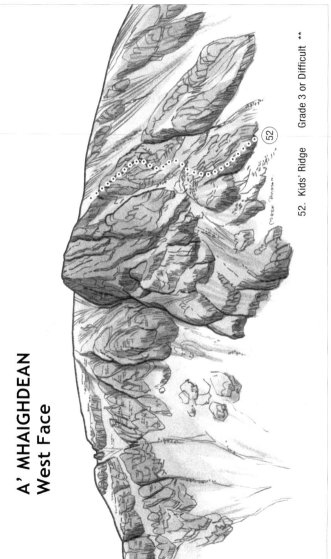

A' MHAIGHDEAN
West Face

52. Kids' Ridge   Grade 3 or Difficult **

53 Gorm Loch Mor Spur   Grade 2   *
Alt 400m   North-East facing   (NG 995 743)   Map p120

Clean slabby ribs on the usual perfect gneiss, but a bit short on character.

Approach

As for Route 52 until 0.5km beyond the head of the Dubh Loch, then go south-west up a stream to reach a bowl west of Gorm Loch Mor. The spur rises directly above the west end of the loch, on the lip of the corrie.

The Route

Go up a delicate slabby rib until it peters out. Go left and up slabs and a short nose, then move right onto more slabs and go up these rightwards. Continue linking slabs until a steeper band crosses the buttress. Climb this left then right. At its top go left to another slabby rib and climb this to the top. The summit is well off to the right across a narrow col.

BEINN LAIR

860m   OS Landranger 19   (NG 981 732)

A mountain of two contrasting faces. On the south-west flank grassy slopes run down to Loch Maree, while the north-east face is huge, dropping in complex 400m cliffs to hidden Gleann Tulacha. Over 20 buttresses stretch for 4km along the glen, with the best climbing being at the west end, notably the classic Very Difficult, Wisdom Buttress. Further left the ridges are mostly scrambling angle, although generally with the odd harder section. The best scrambles are concentrated around the north summit on inward-dipping hornblende schist. All are serious undertakings with escapes ranging from tricky to impossible. The cliffs are quite vegetated and become very greasy when wet, so allow a couple of days of good weather for the cliff to dry out.

54 Tower Ridge   Difficult   *
Alt 450m   North-East facing   (NG 983 738)   Map p120   Diagram p132

A serious and scary route with a sting in the tail. Most of the route is Grade 3, but the crux is exposed and gymnastic, although a one move wonder. The only route in this book where heel hooking is useful!

Approach

From the southern corner of Fionn Loch take the path up towards Bealach Mheinnidh. After 200 metres or so head south-east and pick up a vague path heading through the pass below the north-facing Creag na Gaorach, emerging into the head of Gleann Tulacha (NG 976 746). Beinn Lair dominates the glen, with the broad North Summit Buttress coming lower down the slope than the others. Tower Ridge is the next ridge left, just across a deep gully, with a broad base and a narrow top. Start on the right-hand edge at a stream/gully.

The Route

Go up easy slabs leftwards to grass, with cleaner slabs to the left. Take a grass ledge left onto these (or swing left lower down and climb a pocketed slab, harder). Climb the crest, passing a tower on the right. Where the rib peters out climb a rough outcrop on the right, then slabs and a small crest to the left. A couple of short slabs lead to easy ground level with the foot of a huge leaning tower across the gully to the right.

Go up left to climb clean slabs on the left edge, then grass and more slabs, becoming vegetated at the top. Now move left to broken outcrops on the left arête, with a long low overhang to the right. Zigzag up an awkward steepening, then slabs lead to broken ground below a steep loose wall. Follow a grass ledge right until the overhang stops, then work back up left (greasy) to regain the crest. Broken outcrops and easy slabs lead to a level ridge.

Things now get more serious, and although the next section can be avoided on the left, this is on scarily steep grass and is not recommended. At the neck in the ridge pull up strenuously on overhanging jugs, then follow the exposed arête to another narrow saddle. Go up right of the crest, then cross it and go up a slab to the left skyline. Follow this, bypassing a pinnacle on the right, then cross another pinnacle to a third saddle. The final pinnacle is a dead end, so slant down right from the saddle to an exposed grassy ramp leading into the gully. Regain the ridge, which leads easily to the plateau.

 55 North Summit Buttress   Grade 3   **

Alt 450m   North-East facing   (NG 982 739)   Map p120   Diagram p132

An exciting expedition up a big, serious, intimidating face. Steep at times, but the inward dip of the strata produces numerous good holds. Although the route winds around to avoid the steepest rock it feels a logical line once embarked upon it. Some loose rock in places but spectacular situations.

Approach

As for the previous route to the head of Gleann Tulacha. The described route follows the centre of North Summit Buttress, the lowest on the face, dodging the stepped overhangs at 50m on the left. At the bottom right of the buttress is a steep clean face. A small path traverses left immediately below it and about 100 metres along this the ground opens out. Start here, at a juggy rib, with a big stepped overhang 50m up.

The Route

Climb the rib until steeper rock forces moves left into a minor gully coming down from the big overhang. Go left out of this and up vegetated rock left of the overhang into another minor gully. Go up this (loose), then bear right as soon as possible up onto a grassy step above the big overhang.

Go up left on rough juggy slabs and up an arête. Climb a small overhanging wall on big jugs (or avoid it on the right) to broken ground at half height

CARNMORE

BEINN LAIR
North-East Face

54. Tower Ridge — Difficult *
55. North Summit Buttress — Grade 3 **
56. Butterfly Buttress, L Wing — Moderate

on the buttress. Dodge the next overhang on its left (loose and grassy), then climb a nice spiky rib to easier ground. Climb the right-hand side of the next buttress, finishing by moving left up a pocketed slab onto the nose of the overhang. A shattered arête now leads to more open ground. Go up scrappy rock and grass to reach the left arête of the buttress. Climb this, mostly on jugs, bypassing a steep tower near the top on the left, to arrive at the nicely positioned North Summit.

56 Butterfly Buttress, Left Wing   Moderate
Alt 450m   North-East facing   (NG 979 741)   Map p120   Diagram p132
Steep in places, with a rather indirect line, but nice positions on juggy rock.

Approach
As for the previous two routes as far as the head of Gleann Tulacha. Butterfly Buttress is the double buttress right of North Summit Buttress, between it and the recess of the Amphitheatre. Start on easy slabs below and right of the Left Wing.

The Route
Climb the easy slabs, steeper at the top. Go up left to a broken buttress just left of a deep gully with a steep face on its right. Climb the broken buttress, finishing up juggy black slabs (often wet) to open heathery slopes. Trend left up juggy ribs, aiming for a small steep buttress topped by a prominent perched block. Climb to the block, starting in the chimney down right from it. This takes you to the left arête of the buttress. Carry on up the arête, steep and exposed at first, then easier and quite grassy. When the arête broadens move right and climb the left edge of a central groove, then more jugs above. A central crest now develops as the buttress narrows. Climb this to a pinnacle, dodged on the left (Difficult direct), then an easy ridge leads to the plateau.

CARNMORE

MEALL MHEINNIDH

722m OS Landranger 19 (NG 955 748)

Another mountain of two contrasting flanks, easy on the south-west but with a steep craggy north-east face. This is about 250m high at its maximum and made of hornblende schist with plenty of incut holds.

57 North-East Face   Grade 2
Alt 350m   North-East facing   (NG 957 752)   Map p120   Diagram p134
A fairly easy way up a big face. Indirect and vegetated in places, but with some excellent sections too.

Approach
From Poolewe follow the Carnmore approach described in the introduction until 1km beyond the crossing of the Srathan Buidhe stream. Slant up south-

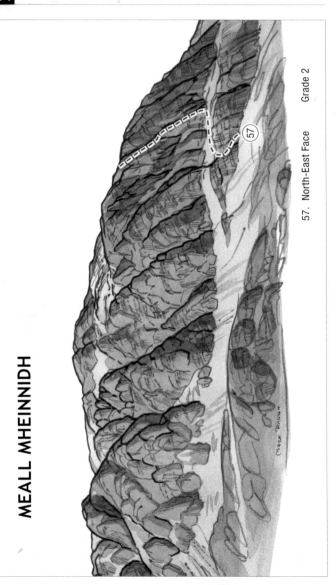

MEALL MHEINNIDH

57. North-East Face   Grade 2

wards to reach the face. There is a steep lower tier, and near the far end of this are two streamlets (just damp streaks in dry weather) with steep rock to their right.

The Route
Start just right of the two streams and follow a weakness slanting left across them. Cleaner rock on their left leads to the terrace above the lower tier. Follow this right for 100m or so until it narrows to a sheep track. Climb slabs above this, then go up left and climb ribs to grass. Carry on up more easy slabs, finishing up a spiky rib. The ground now becomes more broken, with a rake going up left and rows of short ribs right of it. Climb vegetated ribs above, bearing slightly right, with steeper rock up left. Move left onto this when it becomes less steep and go up the slabs. Carry on slightly left and go up a lovely rib on the edge of a gully. More slabs above lead to easy ground. A rib on the right provides a nice finish. A few minor outcrops can be included on the way to the summit.

BEINN AIRIGH CHARR

791m   OS Landranger 19   (NG 930 761)

The western sentinel of the Carnmore area, this superb viewpoint has a north-east summit, Martha's Peak, from which spectacular 400 metre cliffs fall towards Loch an Doire Crionaich. The largest buttress directly above the loch is taken by Ling and Glover's Route, which has a scrappy and vegetated lower half and a steep and serious finish. Left of this and starting much lower down, above the south-east end of the loch, is Bell's Route (which starts up Lower Buttress). Left again is a section of huge boulders topped by the sharp arête of The Beanstalk (HVS), and left again the shorter Square Buttress, above the smaller lochan at NG 940 766.

58 Square Buttress   Difficult
Alt 250m   North-East facing   (NG 938 764)   Map p120   Diagram p136
A steep start leads to slabs of sound juggy rock. Not recommended in the wet.

Approach
Follow the approach from Poolewe described in the introduction as far as Loch an Doire Crionaich. Half a kilometre beyond this is an unnamed lochan, with Square Buttress above. Start at its right-hand edge, where a steep slab leads up leftwards.

The Route
Take the steep slab up left, with the strata sloping unhelpfully. Just to the left a short awkward chimney leads to a grass ledge crossing the buttress. Go right along this, two-thirds of the way to the right-hand edge, then go up steeply on jugs to follow slabs leftwards into the centre of the buttress.

BEINN AIRIGH CHARR

MP Martha's Peak

LB Lower Buttress

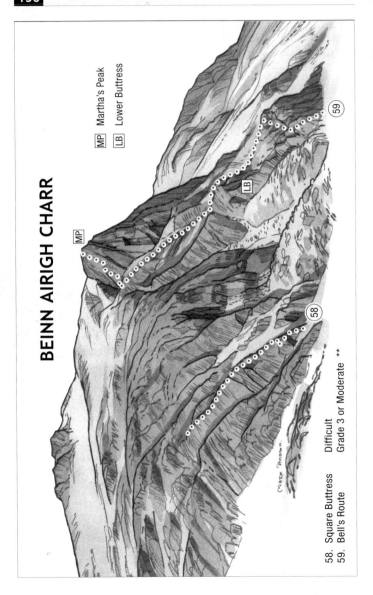

58. Square Buttress   Difficult

59. Bell's Route   Grade 3 or Moderate **

Robin Chalmers high up on Bell's Route (Moderate), Beinn Airigh Charr
Photo: Noel Williams

When the angle eases move right and follow the next ramp up to the top of the main buttress. Go up easy steps above until they run out into the hillside. Easy slabs continue for another 100m or so before petering out to grass.

59 Bell's Route   Grade 3 or Moderate   **

Alt 250m   North-East facing   (NG 935 767)   Map p120   Diagram p136

Slabby, positive and over 400m long, the longest line on the mountain. The top and bottom sections are exposed and worth Moderate, but both can be avoided and the route is not sustained. Not recommended in the wet.

Approach

As for Square Buttress to Loch an Doire Crionaich. The route begins above the south-east end of the loch, and initially ascends a feature called Lower Buttress. Start at the lowest rocks, below and left of an overhanging wall.

The Route

Go up the left-hand edge of the lowest spur, then move right onto the front and up an easy slab. Go up left and then right to a ledge below an overhanging wall. Follow a very narrow ledge left and ascend delicately to the skyline and easy ground. All this lower section can be easily avoided on the left.

Follow easy slabs up right to the crest of the buttress. Climb excellent sharp-edged slabs just left of the crest, then easy ground to a steepening. Climb this right then left on sloping holds, then go up left to the skyline. Continue up easy slabs, then move left and up a steeper rib to arrive on top of Lower Buttress.

Walk across the neck to the main hillside and link together easy slabs to reach an arête with a deep gully on its left. Follow the arête up right, with a nice step off a block, then climb a short vertical wall. Dodge the steeper bits until the arête becomes slabby again and runs out into the hillside.

Cross the gully on the right (Staircase Gully) and climb delicate slabs, gradually easing. Carry on up to a steeper section. This can be avoided on the left, but a spectacular finish is to follow a grassy ramp leading right, then step right onto the main face in an amazingly exposed position. Thankfully big holds lead up to regain the arête, from where easy rocks lead up to the summit of Martha's Peak.

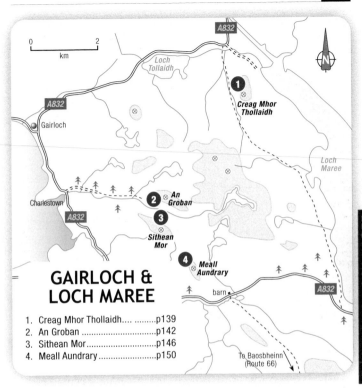

GAIRLOCH & LOCH MAREE

GAIRLOCH AREA

The excellent little peaks behind Gairloch have huge amounts of exposed rock, much of it solid Lewisian gneiss. As well as hundreds of short rock climbs, there is scope for any amount of scrambling, the routes included being merely a sample of the many possibilities available. Their accessibility makes them ideal for an evening, a short day, or a day when the weather is poor on the higher tops. Mountain scrambling on Baosbheinn provides a contrast – really part of Torridon, but most easily accessed from Gairloch.

CREAG MHOR THOLLAIDH

343m   OS Landranger 19   (NG 864 776)

A very rocky hill with lots of short rock climbs on its flanks, including the

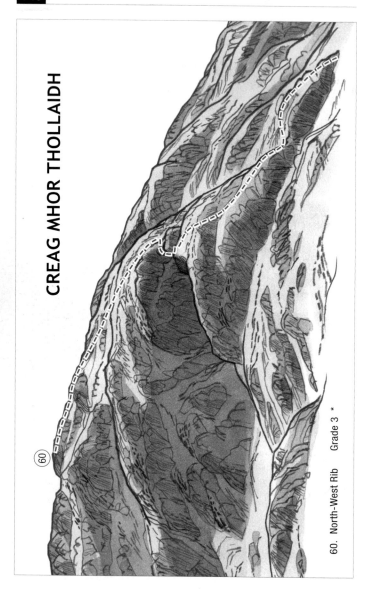

CREAG MHOR THOLLAIDH

60. North-West Rib   Grade 3 *

Iain Thow on North-West Rib (Grade 3), Creag Mhor Thollaidh
Photo: Noel Williams

idyllic Tollie Crags. There is less scrambling than you might expect, as much of the rock is very steep. A superb viewpoint.

60 North-West Rib Grade 3 *
Alt 150m   West facing   (NG 860 780)   Map p139   Diagram p140

A short accessible route ideal for an evening. The rib itself is a good line, but short hard sections force deviations.

Approach
Follow the Tollie to Slattadale path from NG 859 790 past a steep craglet to the foot of the main cliffs. The lowest crag has a steep orange chimney/crack at the bottom. Start just right of this.

The Route
Climb the right-hand edge of the buttress on jugs, then steep slabs to the top of the buttress. Go horizontally left to climb a steep wall with reddish bands on small positive holds, then slabs above lead to an easing. The undercut groove on the right has large loose flakes in it, so avoid it on the left, then climb a rib just left of a heathery groove, above a steep drop on the left. Go up right easily and follow a level heathery ridge to an overhanging nose. Bypass this on the left by steep heather and a traverse right to rejoin the rib.

Climb a groove in the nose above for a few feet until cracked slabs on the left lead to easy ground. Go up to a shelf, climb a broken tier, then bear up left to climb lovely rough slabs crossed by a prominent brown band. Small outcrops lead to the skyline, then go right to twin ribs leading up to the north summit. The main summit lies south-east across a broad saddle. There are easy slabs beyond this on the left-hand side, or alternatively you can go 200 metres right (south-west) from the saddle, descending to reach a clean slabby rib. This is sustained Grade 3, on small holds but with excellent friction, quite exposed near the top.

AN GROBAN

383m   OS Landranger 19   (NG 838 749)

This small pointed peak is prominent behind Gairloch. Both flanks are very rocky, giving endless scrambling possibilities on superb gneiss. ✓ *scro Jun 11 2021*

61 North-West Face   Grade 2/3   *
Alt 200m   West facing   (NG 834 751)   Map p139   Diagram p143

Really two separate scrambles, but they are easily linked to make a good route up the hill. The sloping grain of the rock makes it awkward in places.

Approach
From the Old Inn at the south end of Gairloch follow the private road past Flowerdale House until it ends. Keep ahead past Flowerdale Waterfall. 100 metres beyond this (50 metres before the top bridge) bear left on a rough

AN GROBAN

61. North-West Face   Grade 2/3   *
62. Humpback Buttress   Grade 2   ***
63. Right-Hand Slabs   Grade 2   ***

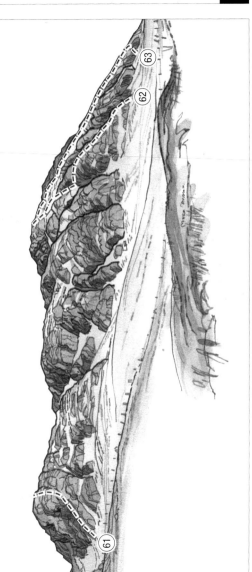

path to a stile. Follow the fence up left then head up rightwards, aiming for a grass slope between two buttresses. The right-hand buttress has two vertical walls. Start on the left-hand edge of the left-hand wall.

The Route

Go up the ridge on the left edge of the wall. At the top keep up left on steeper juggy rock to a minor top. The main peak is up right and easily reached directly, but down and left of this is a large steep grooved wall, home to several rock climbs. Go left to pass under this to the next buttress, which has a steep start and slabs above.

Gain the lowest slab at its bottom left-hand corner and work right across it to the far edge. Move up right onto the higher hanging slab and go up to a niche on the edge of the buttress. Climb the rib above to blocks then go up left to a ledge. Climb the slab above moving left, delicate but always escapable, then climb a gentler slab on the right to easy ground. Various outcrops can be added in on the way to the summit. ✓ *June 2020* *mu*

62 Humpback Buttress   Grade 2   *** ✓ *June 2020* *mu*

Alt 150m   South facing   (NG 837 747)   Map p139   Diagram p143

250m of easy slabs, with the odd harder move, ending on a sharp summit with a great view. The next buttress left also makes a pleasant Grade 2 scramble, but is not as good a line.

Approach

As for Route 61 as far as the stile. Keep ahead up the valley to reach a steep grey wall low on the left-hand slope, leading up to a prominent humped buttress with slabs on its left. Start at the right-hand end of the wall, at its lowest point, about 100 metres before the low drystone wall.

The Route

Go up right of a large block, then bear left to the top of the first buttress. Bear left up heather, boulders and short steps to climb a greasy corner right of a clean rounded nose. Go up left again and climb a steep wall to a large boulder, then easy slabs. Another short steep wall and more slabs lead over the 'Humpback' to a saddle. Straight ahead a shallow gully splits the buttress centrally. Follow slabs right of this, with harder moves if desired. Above these easy steps lead to a short steep wall below a reddish band with a small overhang. Climb this by steep steps from the lowest point on the left (the crack direct through the overhang is Severe). More short outcrops lead up to the summit. BETTER THAN ✓ *Nov 2020* *umu RO*

63 Right-Hand Slabs   Grade 2   *** ✓ *Nov 2020* *umu RO*

Alt 150m   South facing   (NG 838 747)   Map p139   Diagram p143

This is the buttress just right of Humpback Buttress, a sweep of slabs with no strong line but numerous possibilities. The slabs have both incut holds and good friction, so are usually easier than they look.

Iain Thow on Right-Hand Slabs (Grade 2), An Groban
Photo: Noel Williams

Approach
As for Route 62, but carry on until 20 metres beyond the stone wall, just before a grey vertical wall on the left.

The Route
Go up the left-hand chimney/gully left of the vertical wall and carry on up steep steps to a grassy terrace. Link sets of slabs above, delicate in places, until the angle eases. Climb a steepening by an easy left-to-right ramp, then numerous slabs lead up to a large grass shelf below a band of steep red rock. Above a group of small blocks climb a wide stepped weakness between two steeper buttresses, then work up and left linking minor outcrops to the summit.

SITHEAN MOR

384m   OS Landranger 19   (836 740)

Another of the spiky gneiss peaks behind Gairloch, this consists of an east-west ridge with a steep rocky northern flank. Ascents from other directions are possible but are complicated by recent planting and deer fencing. Flowerdale's Sitka spruce plantations have been felled and replaced by native species, part of the attempt to bring back the native Caledonian pine forests.

 64 North Face   Grade 2/3
Alt 150m   North facing   (NG 834 746)   Map p139   Diagram p147

A series of disjointed ribs giving good situations. The grain of the rock dips awkwardly, so the scrambling tends to be harder and less satisfying than on An Groban.

Approach
As for Route 61 to the stile, then cross to the south bank of the stream. Start at the end buttress on the right, the closest to the stream, with a black wall at its top right.

The Route
Easy slabs lead to a steeper buttress. In dry conditions tackle this direct to a halfway shelf, otherwise climb over large pointed blocks to the left, then dodge a steep wall on the left to reach the shelf. An awkwardly grained slab leads to the top of the buttress. Go up two short steep steps, the second either by vertical jugs in the centre (Grade 3) or by an easy left-to-right shelf on the left.

   Go left up heather below an overhanging wall to a wet gully. At the mouth of this go left along a shelf, then follow more heather up left to a large bay. At the back of this climb a shallow rib just right of a wet slot, quite insecure at the top. Go left across a shelf to the crest and up to a steepening. Go left to the skyline, then follow a ramp back up right below a block. Keep going

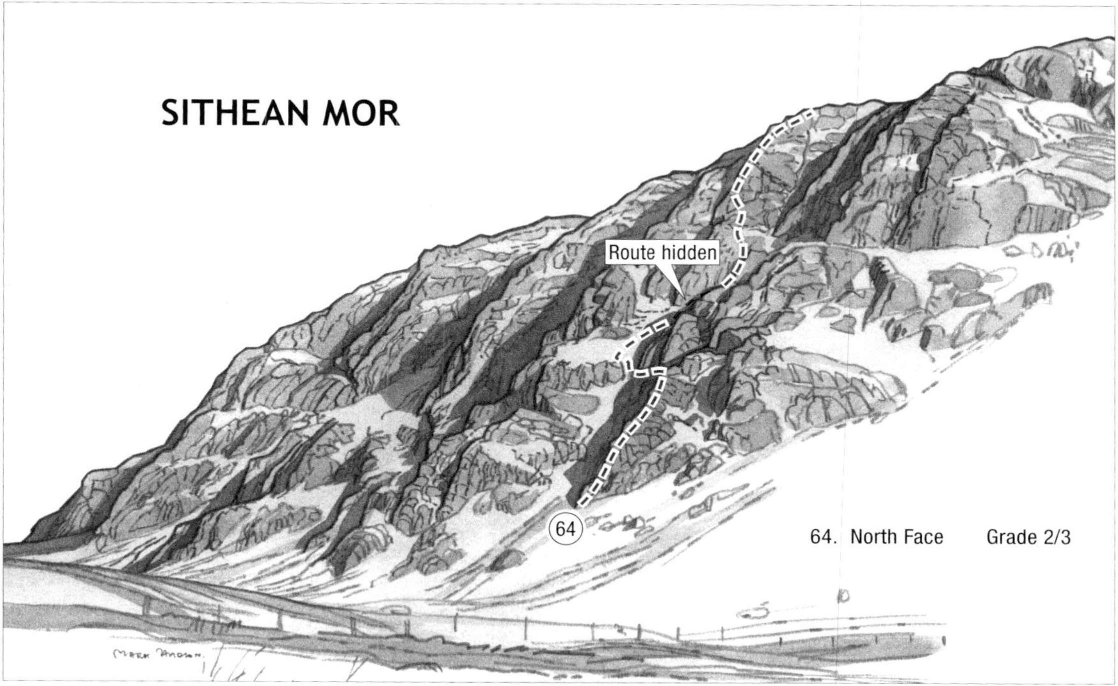

SITHEAN MOR

Route hidden

64. North Face   Grade 2/3

64

MEALL AUNDRARY

65. North-West Buttress   Grade 2/3 **

Noel Williams on North-West Buttress (Grade 2/3), Meall Aundrary
Photo: Iain Thow

right to reach a vertical wall, where steps lead back up left to the ridge again. Follow this up to easy ground. The left-hand summit is the higher, and has a splendid view of the Torridon hills.

MEALL AUNDRARY

327m OS Landranger 19 (NG 846 728)

Accessible scrambling ideal for an evening. The south-east side has many easy-angled slabs which link to give a pleasant Grade 1, but the best route is on the north end of the steep west face.

65 North-West Buttress Grade 2/3 **

Alt 250m   West facing   (NG 845 729)   Map p139   Diagram p148

The right edge of the buttress is a clean rib of rough gneiss, with positive holds making it much easier than it looks.

Approach

Park at a right-hand bend by a small loch at NG 841 721. To the east is the edge of a wood, follow this to its top (there is a path on the west side of the valley, not easy to find on first acquaintance). Carry on up below the west face and slant up below two subsidiary buttresses to reach the large buttress marking the north end of the face. Start on the right-hand corner of this, by an isolated boulder of Torridonian sandstone.

The Route

Climb the rib to a shoulder below a steepening. The groove in the centre is much easier than it looks, but beware the odd loose hold. Carry on to the top of the buttress. Climb a slabby knoll by a Y-shaped groove, then more slabs lead to the skyline. The summit is up on the right, with a couple of steep boulder problems on the way.

BAOSBHEINN

875m OS Landranger 19 (NG 870 654)

A superb hill with a long ridge traverse and numerous cliffs. Most of these are very vegetated, but there is one excellent route.

66 Oidhche Spur Grade 3 **

Alt 550m   North facing   (NG 877 655)   Map p139 & 153   Diagram p151

Sustained rock steps, generally clean, with some exposure and a hard but avoidable crux.

Approach

Take the track south from the barn at NG 857 721 to Loch na h-Oidhche. The new plantations at Bad an Sgalaig are part of the campaign to regenerate the native Caledonian Forest, with ash, rowan, birch, oak and hazel all

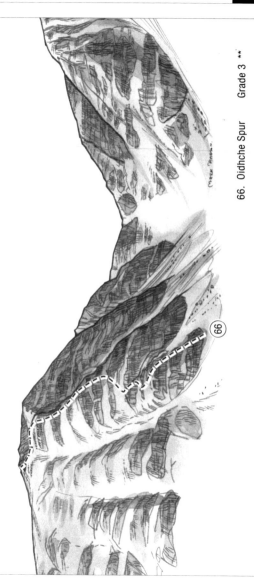

BAOSBHEINN

66. Oidhche Spur   Grade 3 **

⑥⑥

planted. Just before the loch leave the track and go right to a bridge over the outlet stream (unmarked on the 1:50,000 map). Go up south-west to the foot of the face below the south-east peak of Baosbheinn. Start at the right-hand end of the lowest tier of rock in the centre of the face.

The Route
On the right-hand end of the tier is a corner. Start up its left arête then move right to climb the right-hand branch when the corner divides. The arête above leads to easy ground. Go up grass and minor outcrops to a steeper tier, then go left below an overhang and up blocks leftwards to more open ground. Carry on up minor outcrops to a small steep tier, passed by going up left from a rock platform in a central niche. The next tier is hard, but on its extreme right-hand edge a superb rough slab leads to the top of the first section of the spur.

Go up scrappy outcrops, then up right to the skyline, where things get tricky for a few metres. Start on the left and climb an exposed and delicate arête. This can be avoided by an easier rib and corner 5m right. Climb the corner above, finishing on the left arête, then go up blocks to an easing of angle. Carry on up the easy ridge, with the odd outcrop, to a vertical prow. Go right of this up greasy steps until it is possible to step awkwardly left onto the prow. Go up the arête and a short step to easy ground. A pleasant ridge with more short steps carries on past a pinnacle to the summit.

There is more scrambling on the north-west ridge just beyond the main summit (Grade 1). Keep to the crest over the pinnacles, then avoid the steepest descent on the right. If doing this section in reverse the lower arête is excellent, starting at a steep crack on the left, then along the wildly exposed crest.

Elsewhere on the mountain some scrappy scrambling can be found on the end of the north-east ridge, while the left-hand edge of the main face of Creag an Fhithich has some short steep outcrops leading to a narrow ridge. The right-hand rib of the face impresses from a distance, but flatters to deceive.

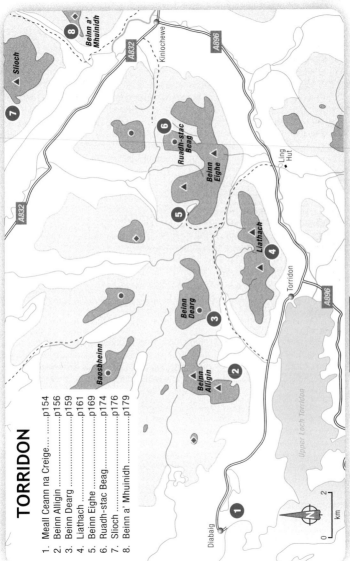

TORRIDON

Diabaig

Baosbheinn

Beinn Alligin

Beinn Dearg

Liathach

Beinn Eighe

Ruadh-stac Beag

Slioch

Beinn a' Mhuinidh

Kinlochewe

Ling Hut

Torridon

Upper Loch Torridon

A832

A896

A896

A832

N

0   km   2

TORRIDON

TORRIDON

A superlative area, with huge amounts of scrambling in a stunning setting. The ridges of Beinn Alligin, Liathach and Beinn Eighe are popular classics, but there are also routes on the more obscure peaks and many good alternative ways up onto the main ridges.

The peaks are largely of Torridonian sandstone capped by quartzite, with the boundary between the two descending eastwards so that the east end of Beinn Eighe is purely quartzite and Beinn Alligin purely sandstone. The sandstone tends to produce steep tiers and blocky pinnacled ridges, while the quartzite often comes in huge sweeps of slabs. At lower levels Meall Ceann na Creige at Diabaig has a lot of excellent scrambling suitable for an evening's exploration, as well as being a well-known climbing ground.

MEALL CEANN NA CREIGE

270m   OS Landranger 24   (NG 804 595)

The hills behind Diabaig may be small, but they are very rocky, with a superb outlook. Better known for its rock climbs, this area also offers excellent scrambling, with the described route just one among many possibilities.

 67 West Spur   Grade 3   **
Alt sea level   West facing   (NG 799 596)   Map p153   Diagram p155
Sea to summit on slabby gneiss outcrops with very little walking in between. Intimidating in places, but with lots of possible escapes.

Approach
From the road end at Diabaig pier follow the shoreline along until stopped by a steep spur with slabs to its left. A new fence has made access to the bottom quite convoluted at high tide, so better to wait and savour the superb setting, after all this is the land where mañana is much too frantic a concept!

The Route
Go up the easy-angled but delicate slabs, then right up steps to a small rowan. Climb the blocky rib above this to a wide terrace. Up left is a steep rib, gained by a right-to-left weakness, steep but on good holds. Climb blocks above, then go left through trees and up a small slab to a heathery niche on the next rib. Go up steeply to more heather, then easy slabs lead up left to a terrace and the path.

A steep wall lies ahead, avoided by a vegetated right-slanting groove a few metres left. Continue up right, then climb a short steep crack and easy slabs to another large terrace. The spur above is too steep, so avoid it by a greasy rib in the gully on the right. Go up left onto the slabs above the steep section. Climb these, breaking through the intimidating bulge above by a right-to-left weakness, much easier than it looks. More slabs lead to another

DIABAIG
Meall Ceann na Creige

67. West Spur   Grade 3 **

Sections in gully

67

West Spur, Meall Ceann na Creige, Diabaig. Photo: Iain Thow

bulge. This is about Very Difficult, so go off right into the gully, returning about 10m higher. Follow a ledge round onto the front of the buttress and go up this to an easing. Slabs lead to the top of the cliff, with more slabs and problems on the short distance to the summit.

BEINN ALLIGIN

986m OS Landranger 24 (NG 865 612)

This distinctive mountain gives a classic traverse, with easy but exposed scrambling over the Horns. The flanks contain a lot of rock, but their tiered nature produces few scrambles.

68 Tom na Gruagaich, Na Fasreidhnean Grade 1
Alt 450m East facing (NG 862 591) Map p153

The south rim of Coir' nan Laogh makes an enjoyable alternative to the path. Much easier than it looks.

Approach
From the car park at the foot of Coire Mhic Nobuil (NG 869 577) take the path on the west side of the stream leading directly up towards Beinn Alligin. Follow this to the foot of Coir' nan Laogh.

The Route
Go up left to the skyline, where a minor path leads up short bouldery steps.

At a steeper prow climb a slab to its right, then a steep groove and a short wall. The path avoids the first two on the right and the third on the left. Easy scrambling along the line of the path now leads to a grassy ridge.

69 Horns of Alligin   Grade 1/2   **
Alt 750m   (NG 876 612)   Map p153

A jagged ridge with some easy scrambling over its three summits, mostly on an obvious path.

Approach
From the car park at the foot of Coire Mhic Nobuil (NG 869 577) follow the path up the east bank of the stream. Fork left just after crossing the stream to head up towards the Bealach a' Chomhla. Soon after crossing the Allt a' Bhealaich a steep path (with some easy scrambling) branches up leftwards onto a shoulder, then up to the Horns.

The Route
Go up a few short rock steps to the first Horn, then zigzag down left of the crest. The second Horn can be taken either direct or via an easier zigzag on the left. The third Horn is tackled direct by a steep chimney. At the cairn bear left and descend steeply, either direct or via a path on the left. At a gap the pinnacle ahead is usually avoided on the left, but can be easily included at the price of a few awkward steps at the far end. A few minor bits of scrambling can also be found on the ascents to Sgurr Mhor and Tom na Gruagaich.

70 Backfire Ridge   Grade 2
Alt 600m   North facing   (NG 875 617)   Map p153   Diagram p158

A good line with a wild and remote feel. Sustained at Grade 1 with the odd harder move and some airy positions. Greasy in the wet, with some loose rock.

Approach
As for Route 69 to the Allt a' Bhealaich, then carry on along the lower path to reach the Bealach a' Chomhla. At the lochans just beyond the pass head up left to reach a rocky shelf just east of Loch Toll nam Biast. From here the ridge leading up to the highest of the Horns is obvious, but the way onto it isn't.

The Route
Pass the first low rock tier to reach flat slabs and go up to a larger vertical tier. Follow a shelf left below this until above the Bealach a' Chomhla, where the angle of the face above eases. Climb the first section by steep steps, the next by slabs, and a third hidden section by a right-to-left ramp at its left-hand end. The angle now eases below the ridge proper.

Scramble up steep piles of blocks right of the grassy runnel running up the centre of the ridge. As the ridge narrows the runnel itself is used in a couple

TORRIDON

BEINN ALLIGIN
The Horns of Alligin

70. Backfire Ridge   Grade 2

of places. The ridge levels out and small easy towers and one steeper one lead to a grassy shelf below a long tier. This can be climbed on the right on steep jugs, but the finish is very loose and better avoided. The next tier is taken direct, then a jutting nose gained from the right provides a good finish, arriving by the summit cairn on the third Horn.

BEINN DEARG

914m OS Landranger 19 (NG 895 608)

Often neglected in favour of its larger neighbours, Beinn Dearg overlooks some tremendous wild country. As well as the two routes described, the north-west ridge of Stuc Loch na Cabhaig has a few easy steps on a nice airy ridge, while the obvious step in the main ridge consists of two steep blocks passed by central cracks, then a narrow bouldery arête (Grade 1).

71 South-West Face   Grade 3
Alt 550m   South-West facing   (NG 890 607)   Map p153   Diagram p160

A succession of boulder problems adding interest to a steep ascent, all avoidable. The main frontal face is similar, but with steeper and often wetter faces.

Approach

As for Route 69 to the Allt a' Bhealaich, then stay on the east side of the stream and slant up to the foot of the face. Start on the left-hand edge of the third gully left of the main frontal face.

The Route

Work up left, including outcrops as desired until the buttress gets more defined. Here a steep band crosses it, with a choice of cracks and arêtes on perfect rock. Another steep step then leads to a third with a pinnacle. Climb this and step off the top. There are several more steps before the buttress peters out into grassy slopes leading up to the summit.

72 Carn na Feola, North Ridge   Difficult   *
Alt 400m   North facing   (NG 917 617)   Map p153

Steep tiers of sandstone in a remote setting with a sting in the tail. A serious route, although the hard bits are short.

Approach

From the Coire Dubh car park (NG 958 569) follow the path up between Liathach and Beinn Eighe, forking right onto the path to Coire Mhic Fhearchair. Where this turns east go down north-west and cross rough ground past Loch nan Cabar to the vertical foot of the North Ridge. The route can be reached up broken ground to the left of this, but better is to follow the foot of the cliff up rightwards until above the first two tiers. A narrow grass ledge then leads left below another vertical tier.

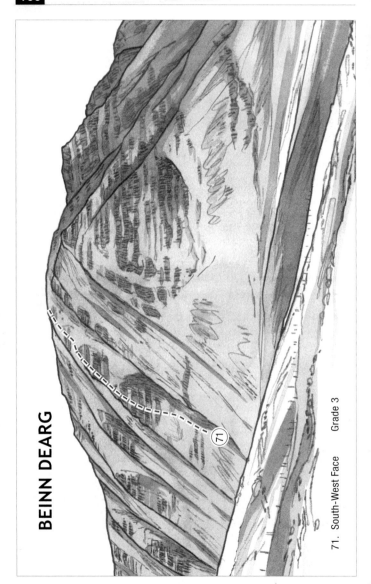

BEINN DEARG

71. South-West Face   Grade 3

The Route

Keep going left until the tier above shrinks to only 5m or so, then climb any of several weaknesses. Work back rightwards up grass and short steps to a band of steep clean slabs directly above the nearest point of Lochan Carn na Feola. Zigzag up these near the right-hand end. More small outcrops lead to a larger greasy tier. Start below an overhang (hard) and move up left (or avoid the tier further right). Above is a smooth curving scoop, climbed by a right-slanting weakness. Carry on up, passing right of a greasy tower, then moving left up blocks.

The ridge narrows below a steeper tier, climbed on the arête by steep blocks. The top move is scary, but there is a useful hidden jug round to the right (this tier can be avoided by going a long way left). The next tier is climbed by a niche with a hard start and a wide bridge to finish. Blocks left of a prow then lead to a large terrace. The vertical cliff beyond this is climbed on its left arête by a wide crack. This is quite strenuous, but with good sharp holds in the crack. It can be avoided by going a long way left. Easier rocks now lead to the top.

LIATHACH

1055m   OS Landranger 25   (NG 929 579)

A contender for the grandest hill in Scotland, the summit ridge is a classic scramble, exposed but not hard, and its flanks contain numerous other possibilities.

 73 Mullach an Rathain, South Ridge   Grade 2   ✷✷

Alt 650m   South facing   (NG 911 569)   Map p153   Diagram p163

A well-positioned scramble leading to Liathach's western summit.

Approach

From the road at NG 914 554 follow the path up the west side of the Allt an Tuill Bhain (past brilliant bouldering) into the hollow of Toll Ban, then bear left to a shoulder. The rock tier below the shoulder offers some scrappy Grade 2 scrambling following vegetated ribs, steep at first, then easy.

The Route

At the first rock band go up a gully a few metres left of a detached block (several harder alternatives). Easy steps lead to a grassy groove in the middle of the ridge. The rocks on either side are more fun, first right, then left. Go up right to climb steeper rocks, with the path giving easy options, then zigzag up to cross an exposed narrow arête (path on the right). Pass an overhanging pinnacle by a groove on the left to reach a level ridge, then go up boulders to a tower, also passed on the left to reach easy ground with surprising suddenness.

TORRIDON

Noel Williams on the Am Fasarinen Traverse (Grade 2), Liathach
Photo: Iain Thow

74 Am Fasarinen Traverse   Grade 2   ***
Alt 900m   (NG 925 575)   Map p153   Diagram p163

This lovely pinnacled ridge links Liathach's two Munros, giving airy positions without too much difficulty. A path along ledges on the south side misses all the fun (but is still exposed). The ridge is usually done east to west, but west to east gives better scrambling. Both ways are described.

West to East: From the first col (the escape path goes off right here) go up easy steps, then climb two towers direct (or dodge them on the right). Cross the summit, descend steeply and pass right of a flat-topped tower. A steep ascent leads to two level sections, then the ridge bends left and right. Descend a steep shattered gully on the right, then go left and rejoin the ridge. Drop to a col and traverse to another col, then climb the next large tower direct. This is steep at the top, easily avoided by a path on the right. Keep on the ridge across another notch and summit, then over blocks to drop to a col. The final two towers can be climbed direct or avoided on the right. An exposed knife-edged descent leads to easy ground.

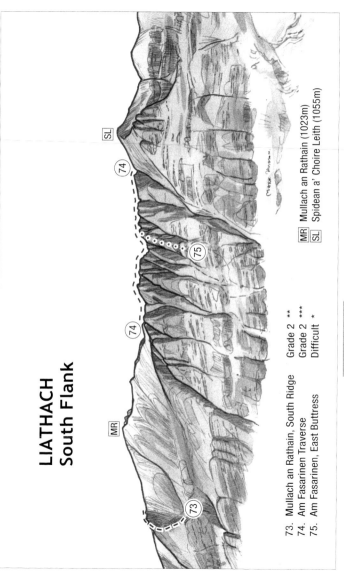

LIATHACH
South Flank

MR Mullach an Rathain (1023m)
SL Spidean a' Choire Leith (1055m)

73. Mullach an Rathain, South Ridge   Grade 2 **
74. Am Fasarinen Traverse   Grade 2 ***
75. Am Fasarinen, East Buttress   Difficult *

TORRIDON

East to West: From the first col either dodge the first two pinnacles by a path on the left, or go over them direct (exposed start and steep descents). From the notch beyond go over a blocky top, pass left of the next summit, then descend to another notch. Follow the ridge over the next top, descending to join a good path on the left. Carry on down to a col and traverse to another col. Go up broken ground on the ridge before traversing left to climb a shattered gully. Stay on the crest over two level sections, down to a notch, then over a flat-topped tower and up steeply to reach the main summit. The final section has two steep descents on the crest, both easily avoided on the left.

75 Am Fasarinen, East Buttress   Difficult   *
Alt 750m   South facing   (NG 926 574)   Map p153   Diagram p163

A serious and quite technical route with a spectacular finish.

Approach
Either traverse westwards from the usual ascent path up Liathach, or descend steeply from the main ridge. For the former route follow the well-used path up the Allt an Doire Ghairbh from the layby at NG 936 566 into Toll a' Meitheach. Where the path goes up right below the top tier of cliffs leave it and traverse left below the upper cliffs. Go up a short groove about 10m left of the waterfall coming out of Coire Liath Mor (cairn at the top). Slant up left to the skyline then traverse left below the steeper rock of Pyramid Buttress to the open corrie south-west of the summit.

Descend slightly to a stream junction, then continue left on a broad sloping terrace to reach the top one of two prominent scree patches (smaller patch just beyond). If the ledge you are on becomes narrow, go back and take a lower one – the correct ledge is wide, with a well-used deer path, other ledges are dead ends. Start 45 degrees up right from the highest point of the upper scree patch, at the foot of the first rock band that completely crosses the buttress.

This same point can be reached by descending steeply from the col at the east end of the Fasarinen Pinnacles to reach the stream junction referred to above at about 750m. The top part of the route (by far the best bit) can be easily reached from the lowest col on the Fasarinen ridge. Descend 30m or so, then take a wide but steeply sloping grass ledge eastwards. Slant up on the upper branch of this to arrive at the skyline below the steep final tier of the route.

The Route
Climb a corner with an overhanging right wall until forced left to a grassy groove. Exit right to grass, then climb serious vegetated ground to the top of the tier. On the next tier climb a steep groove with a prominent crack in its left wall, swing right onto a nose and go up to the top. More small tiers follow, one with a neat little face climbed by a thin Y-crack (Very Difficult but easily avoided). Climb the next big tier by a groove on the left, a hard

Iain Thow soloing East Buttress (Difficult), Am Fasarinen, Liathach
Photo: Noel Williams

start leading to good open scrambling up a ridge. On the next tier climb a square-cut groove on the left, exiting right to a shelf, then go up to the large top tier. This is serious and committing but can be avoided by the large open gully on the left. Go up left on scrappy ground to a narrow grass ledge at one-third height. Step right to climb the right-hand of two mossy grooves to blocks and a small ledge. Finish up a prominent steep corner on big holds, a strenuous grand finale. Equally good is to move further right to a platform on the arête and finish airily up this.

 76 Stuc a' Choire Dhuibh Bhig, East Ridge   Grade 1 or 2
Alt 700m   East facing   (NG 945 585)   Map p153

Only minor scrambling, but a good line up the hill.

Approach
From the Coire Dubh car park (NG 958 569) follow the path northwards up to about 330m. Go left up walking-angle slabs, then steeper boulders to heather. Traverse right to reach the ridge above the first tier of steep dank rock. Carry on up the ridge to a short scramble near the top.

The Route
Climb the first tier by a steep chimney left of the arête then the second by a tower of blocks, both Grade 2. Easier options exist nearby. Quartzite boulders lead to the summit of Stuc a' Choire Dhuibh Bhig.

 77 Spidean a' Choire Leith, North Ridge   Grade 1/2
Alt 800m   North facing   (NG 927 583)   Map p153

A slog to reach, but a nice airy upper ridge.

Approach
From the Coire Dubh car park (NG 958 569) follow the path up between Liathach and Beinn Eighe, and from the fork on the pass bear left (south-west) up very rough ground to reach the broad foot of the ridge between Coire na Caime and Coire Dubh Mor.

The Route
There are a few problems near the bottom, then a long steep grass slope (traces of a path) leads to two steeper tiers. Climb a central blocky rib on the first, with a similar rib above. Climb the second by steep blocks just left of a flying buttress. The ridge now eases, with all difficulties avoidable on the right. Following the true arête gives three steep prows and some enjoyable easy ridge, all with huge drops on the left.

 78 PC Buttress   Difficult   *
Alt 700m   North facing   (NG 921 577)   Map p153   Diagram p167

A good line and good rock, although with the odd loose block. Steep and serious, with a hard crux and some exposure. Probably the hardest route in this guide.

LIATHACH
Coire na Caime

78. PC Buttress

79. Northern Pinnacles

Difficult *

Moderate **

TORRIDON

Approach

From the Lochan in Coire na Caime, usually approached as for Route 77, PC Buttress is directly above, dividing the upper corrie in two. Go up right to a rock terrace below the preliminary tiers in front of the buttress.

The Route

Climb a slabby rib in the centre of the lowest tier, then a groove in the nose above. Climb the next tier by steep steps right of the central weakness. The angle now eases and broken rock leads to the start of the main buttress. Climb a weakness just left of the tallest section of the tier, then walk left up steps and grooves to a grassy terrace.

The next section is the crux, and is hard for the grade, but can be avoided by unpleasant vegetated ground further left. Climb a delicate slab right of overhangs to the next terrace. You are now committed! Follow grooves up left then take a ledge horizontally right to a prominent huge block. Bridge up behind the block then work up left to the skyline, where the route eases.

Continue up the crest to a terrace, then go up a slabby nose right of a mossy groove and up to a level section of ridge. A large flake blocks the way, climbed airily on its crest. Another slabby tier now leads to easy ground and a subsidiary top. Easy steps link this with the main ridge.

79 Northern Pinnacles   Moderate   **

Alt 700m   North-East facing   (NG 918 581)   Map p153   Diagram p167

A serious and exposed route, especially by the direct version. The hardest part of the pinnacles themselves can be avoided, making a Grade 3 version if the approach from upper Coire na Caime is used.

Approach

These form the western bounding ridge of Coire na Caime, usually reached as for Route 77. The pinnacles themselves are most easily approached from the upper south-west corner of Coire na Caime, but can also be reached via a steep grassy rake on the north face of Meall Dearg or by the direct version described.

The Route

From the lochan in Coire na Caime avoid the first cliff on the left to reach the second steep tier. Climb a small preliminary tier, then take a left-slanting weakness close under the steep face. This is harder than it looks and quite exposed at the top (detours left help in places). Reach a large grass shelf, go up right and climb a short steep groove. Big but greasy steps now lead up left. At the top of these go up right to the ridge. Follow this up better rock with short problems until it eases. Cross a minor summit and at the col beyond dodge the pinnacles on the right. Go up to an easing then follow the arête over the summit of Meall Dearg.

At the next col the easy approach from upper Coire na Caime comes in from the left. Take the first easy pinnacle direct, then the second by a slab and steps on the right, finishing up a gully. The third and longest pinnacle is taken direct, sometimes using a groove to the left, finishing up a greasy chimney on the right. The fourth pinnacle is started direct, then for the Grade 3 version go right along ledges to finish up a short chimney. For the direct finish go up left to an exposed move onto a slab (hard if damp). Above this there is another airy pull up before the ridge eases.

BEINN EIGHE

1010m   OS Landranger 19 & 25   (NG 951 611)

A complete range in itself rather than a single peak, Beinn Eighe's northern corries provide several excellent steep routes on square-cut quartzite. The complete traverse of the mountain is a classic day out which includes a couple of sections of easy scrambling.

 80 Lawson, Ling & Glover's Route   Grade 2   *
Alt 650m   North facing   (NG 938 609)   Map p153   Diagram p170
A slog to start, but an enjoyable clamber up a blocky ridge higher up.

Approach
From Coire Dubh car park (NG 958 569) take the path up between Liathach and Beinn Eighe. Fork right to go round into Coire Mhic Fhearchair. At the loch go steeply right up scree to the mouth of a large gully.

The Route
Go up easy rock steps just right of the gully, then slog up steep grass, heading for a blocky rib centrally placed on the slope to the right. Go up this, then continue in the same line to reach the ridge just above a small blunt pinnacle. Follow the bouldery ridge until it narrows, then climb a stepped groove in the arête (the only unavoidable Grade 2 section on the route). Now climb either a series of problems on the left or easier broken ground to the right. Climb a steeper tower to a flattening, then more rounded towers before the ridge slackens off into boulders leading up to Sail Mhor.

 81 Ceum Grannda   Grade 2   *
Alt 900m   West facing   (NG 941 601)   Map p153   Diagram p170
Short and sweet – an airily positioned ridge scramble.

Approach
On the ridge between Coinneach Mhor and Sail Mhor, usually descended from the former as part of a traverse of the main ridge, but easily reached over Sail Mhor by the scramble described above.

The Route
A preliminary clamber over blocks and through a cleft pinnacle leads to a small col. Climb any of three steep corners, then continue up an open slab (gained more easily from the right). Finish up a bouldery ridge. In descent the lower corners can be awkward.

TORRIDON

BEINN EIGHE
Coire Mhic Fhearchair

80. Lawson, Ling & Glover's Route   Grade 2 *
81. Ceum Grannda   Grade 2 *
82. East Buttress   Difficult ***

82 Coire Mhic Fhearchair, East Buttress Difficult ***
Alt 700m North facing (NG 946 603) Map p153 Diagram p170

A superb line in a magnificent situation. Steep, exposed, intimidating and serious, but covered in positive holds. Perhaps the best route of its grade in Scotland.

Approach
As for Route 80 to Coire Mhic Fhearchair. The route is the left-hand of the Triple Buttresses that dominate the corrie. The lower sandstone section is steep, wet and best avoided. Traverse in from the left along Broad Terrace, at the base of the quartzite tier. Some easy scrambling can be found on the way up to the left end of the terrace and there is one scary step halfway along. Start 10 metres left of where Broad Terrace reaches East Central Gully.

The Route
Climb a steep open groove on big square-cut holds, then move right and go up a crack in the gully wall. Return to the crest and go up easily to a terrace. Climb the crest to another shelf, then go up left into a steep shattered area and out onto the front of the buttress. Climb this (easiest right of centre). It is steep and exposed, but still on good holds. Alternatively there is a less airy but very steep corner round to the right. The angle now eases off and short steps lead up to the plateau.

83 Stuc Coire an Laoigh, East Ridge Grade 1
Alt 750m East facing (NG 970 592) Map p153

Although the scrambling doesn't amount to much, the ridge provides an enjoyable alternative to the path slogging up the headwall of Coire an Laoigh.

Approach
Follow the path up from the small wood at NG 977 578 to the 650m contour. Bear up left to reach the ridge.

The Route
The ridge is broad at first, with boulders and walking-angle slabs. Halfway up it narrows, and here a steeper slab is climbed centrally by a short groove. An exposed step down just right of the arête then leads to broken ground and mossy slabs. Follow these airily along the narrow ridge to the pointed summit of Stuc Coire an Laoigh. Continue round the ridge to rejoin the path at the col.

84 Spidean Coire nan Clach, North Ridge Grade 2 **
Alt 700m North-East facing (NG 970 603) Map p153 Diagram p173

Easy-angled quartzite slabs with overlaps. Much of this could be walked up by the confident, but it is quite smooth in places and the overlaps add exposure. The described line is just one among many choices, and all difficulties are avoidable.

Approach

The ridge rises above Lochan Uaine (unnamed on the 1:50,000 map) on the saddle south of Ruadh-stac Beag (NG 968 605). This is best reached from Kinlochewe, either over Ruadh-stac Beag or up the corrie between it and the east end of Beinn Eighe. From the lochan go leftwards below steep cliffs to reach broken slabs and scree right of the stream descending from the upper corrie between Spidean Coire nan Clach and Sgurr Ban.

The Route

Link together minor slabs until the rock becomes more continuous. Keep to the main rib line until it reaches overlaps coming in from the left. Climb a delicate slab right of a right-facing corner, then bear right to a smooth slab below a larger overlap. Traverse right across the bottom of this and climb its right-hand edge, then the narrower inset slab above. Go up left of a cairn and through shattered overlaps. Head for a short steep band on the skyline and go through a notch in it, then easy slabs lead up the ridge, with a pleasantly narrow arête leading to the summit.

85 Toll Ban Headwall   Grade 2

Alt 800m   North facing   (NG 978 600)   Map p153   Diagram p173

A scenic approach into one of the area's wildest corries leads to a short but sound scramble up slabs. Inward-dipping strata give sharp positive holds.

Approach

From the parking place just off the road at NH 021 628 a good path leads up to the saddle between Meall a'Ghiubhais and the main Beinn Eighe group. Head up southwards and follow the stream up to Loch an Tuill Bhain at NG 978 603 (unnamed on the 1:50,000 map). Go up broken rock and scree to the lowest point of the slabs below the col between Sgurr Ban and Sgurr nan Fhir Duibhe.

The Route

Climb two corners and a blunt rib to a grassy niche. From the top of the niche go straight up to reach a bigger steeper nose. Climb a smaller nose to its right. Either finish easily above or go 10 metres right to nice slabs finishing just below the col.

86 The Black Carls   Grade 1   *

Alt 950m   (NG 983 603)   Map p153

An airy scramble along a narrow shattered arête.

Approach

Usually reached by the path from Cromasaig (NH 025 610). Follow this up to the fork in the Allt a' Chuirn then go straight up the ridge ahead to the summit of Creag Dhubh. Follow the ridge south-west to reach the pinnacles.

The Route

Either climb the first tower steeply, or pass it on the right. Weave in and out

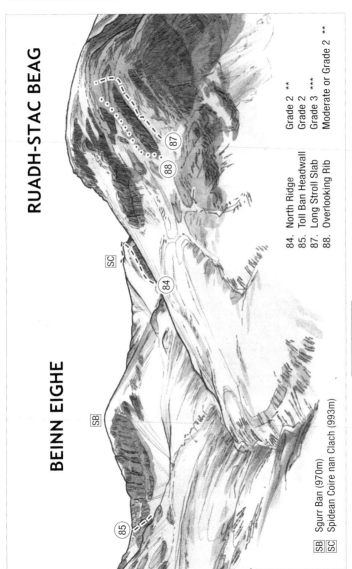

RUADH-STAC BEAG

BEINN EIGHE

SB Sgurr Ban (970m)
SC Spidean Coire nan Clach (993m)

84. North Ridge — Grade 2 **
85. Toll Ban Headwall — Grade 2
87. Long Stroll Slab — Grade 3 ***
88. Overlooking Rib — Moderate or Grade 2 **

TORRIDON

of smaller pinnacles and down to the next col. Go up a corner, then follow an easy narrow ridge. At the next notch either climb steeply just left of the arête or take an easy path on the left. At the final notch either climb direct or use a broken path on the left before regaining the crest by a short gully.

RUADH-STAC BEAG

896m OS Landranger 19 (NG 972 613)

Hidden away behind Beinn Eighe, Ruadh-stac Beag is quite an independent summit – steep and rocky all round. Most of it is very shattered, but the clean quartzite slabs at the north-east corner give a couple of excellent scrambles.

87 Long Stroll Slab Grade 3 ***
Alt 600m East facing (NG 977 617) Map p153 Diagram p173

Quite intimidating but not at all hard. More direct versions are feasible, one of which is the Very Difficult rock climb The Long Stroll.

Approach

As for Route 85 to the saddle between Meall a' Ghiubhais and the main Beinn Eighe group. Head up south-west and cross the Allt Toll a' Ghiubhais. The 100m triangular slab is obvious, at the north-east foot of the mountain. Start centrally, at the lowest point.

The Route

Go up to a right-facing corner and follow this and its left-hand arête. Below and left of the main overlap is a smaller shattered overlap stretching leftwards. Traverse left below this until it eases, then go back up right into the centre of the slab above the overlaps. Now go up direct, keeping right of the blanker part of the slab, delicate in places. When the slab ends at a scree shoulder go left up juggy ribs to broken ground. A few more minor outcrops can be found on the way to the summit. The strange metal cage close to the summit is to protect a rare moss.

88 Overlooking Rib Moderate or Grade 2 **
Alt 600m East facing (NG 977 616) Map p153 Diagram p173

This is the rib overlooking the left-hand edge of Long Stroll Slab. The start is steep and sustained, but can be avoided by a diversion left, returning across loose scree. The top half is nice and airy. There are some awkward moves and some exposure, but not together.

Approach

As for the previous route. Start at the bottom of the rib bounding the slab on its left.

The Route

Climb the rib just right of the crest to reach a grassy ledge. Go up left from this to gain the crest (crux). Follow the crest up over another steepening,

Noel Williams on Long Stroll Slab (Grade 3), Ruadh-stac Beag
Photo: Iain Thow

easier than it looks, to reach ledges leading up right to the edge overlooking Long Stroll Slab.

An easier start (Grade 2) is to begin at the left-hand end of a scree shelf below the rib and go up broken slabs, heading up leftwards below steeper slabs until you meet the screes on the left. Climb a short tier to scree above the first level of cliffs. Traverse right across this (horrible) to reach the edge overlooking Long Stroll Slab.

Climb the airy rib above. Gradually the angle eases before a final flourish up a blocky nose of knobbly Pipe Rock. Minor outcrops can be found above.

SLIOCH

981m   OS Landranger 19   (NH 004 690)

The square-cut tower of Slioch dominates the east side of Loch Maree, its ascent from Kinlochewe being a classic walk. The north-west buttress provides an enjoyable way of turning this into a loop.

89 North-West Buttress   Grade 2 or 3   **
Alt 600m   West facing   (NG 999 691)   Map p153   Diagram p177

Open scrambling with much variation possible in a splendid situation. Not particularly exposed and a good choice for a mixed-ability group.

Approach
From Incheril (NH 038 624) follow the track north-west and along Loch Maree to the bridge at the foot of Gleann Bianasdail. Carry on north-west to the waterfall and deserted settlement at NH 003 670. Head up north-west following the stream to a prominent boulder on the watershed below the north-west corner of Slioch's cliffs. The scramble takes the ridge directly above, avoiding the initial steep section.

The Route
Above are twin buttresses. Either start right of the right-hand one and traverse onto it at 5m, then climb the ridge above on good holds (Grade 3), or go up the gully between the buttresses and right onto the top of the steep section at 30m.

From a grass ledge go up right and up the right-hand side of a spur, then the right-hand side of the prow above. Carry on up clean outcrops to an open slope. Above this go up left of two rounded pinnacles, then up left to the skyline. Climb clean slabby rock, go right of a prow, then up the slabs behind it and stacked blocks above. Carry on up the crest, climbing a short steeper wall by a groove.

The buttress now becomes a sharp ridge, and a short exposed descent leads to two easy pinnacles. A steep path with small outcrops now leads to the summit, or alternatively an exposed ledge leads left again across the far wall of the gully to the skyline of Main Buttress, which provides a spectacular finish (Grade 2).

SLIOCH
North-West Flank

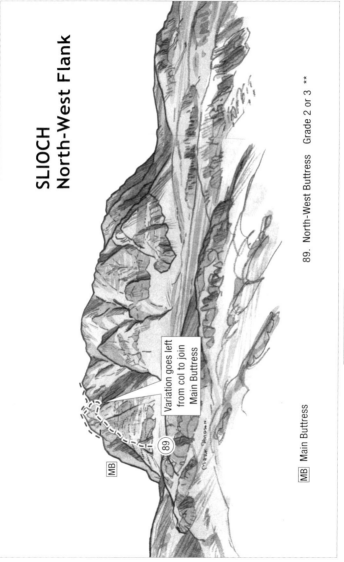

MB Main Buttress

89. North-West Buttress   Grade 2 or 3 **

Variation goes left from col to join Main Buttress

89

MB

BEINN A' MHUINIDH
Bonnaidh Donn

goat track

90

90. Route One   Difficult **

Those coming up the usual route from Gleann Bianasdail can find some easy scrambling on the way up Sgurr Dubh. From the two lochans beyond this go left to climb an easy-angled broken rib to the main summit area (Grade 2). Alternatively the slabs low down on the north side of the east ridge of Sgurr an Tuill Bhain at NH 026 687 provide some entertainment with a remote atmosphere.

BEINN A' MHUINIDH

692m   OS Landranger 19   (NH 031 660)

Although the summit of the hill is anonymous moorland, the line of cliffs on the north-west and south-west flanks provides plenty of character, culminating in the steep clean face of the Bonnaidh Donn.

90 Bonnaidh Donn, Route One   Difficult   **
Alt 400m   West facing   (NH 022 655)   Map p153   Diagram p178

Steep clean quartzite ribs, exposed in places, but with good positive holds.

Approach
From Incheril (NH 038 624) follow the track north-west for 3km as far as the stream descending from the large waterfall. Head up steeply to reach the main rock band at a beak of rock seen on the skyline as you approach (this is not the beak of rock mentioned in the Northern Highlands climbing guide). A goat track leads left below the cliff and in a few hundred metres you reach another beak of rock where the face bends right. This is the first point at which you can see all the way up Gleann Bianasdail.

The Route
Start just left of the beak and go right up a slab to the skyline. Carry on up the crest to easier ground. Go up right to climb a steep face, starting at a large block. An easy rib on the left leads to a steeper thin rib on the right. Carry on easily to another steep rib, which is started on its left, then climbed on the right-hand side of the arête. Where the next rib curves over rightwards go left to an intimidatingly steep rib, the crux of the route. Climb it by a groove just left of the arête, stepping right onto the skyline near the top. Above this a small overhang and an easy rib lead to the plateau.

Route Two to the left is also graded Difficult, but is much harder than Route One. Right of Route One the face is more broken, and there are many scrambling possibilities between there and the steeper routes by the waterfall.

TORRIDON

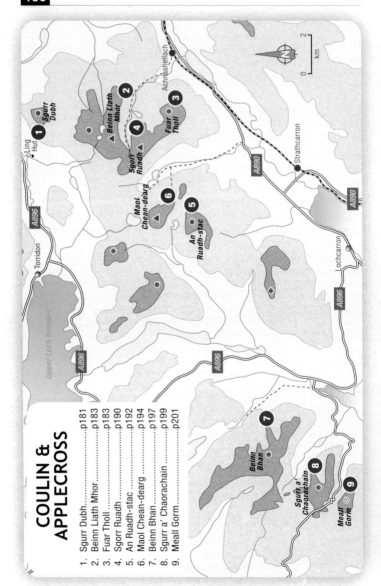

COULIN &
APPLECROSS

COULIN TO APPLECROSS

Bounded by the deep trenches of Glen Torridon and Strath Carron, this area has a clutch of individual peaks, all quite distinctive in character. All of them have large amounts of rock too broken for good rock climbing but which can provide excellent scrambling. Some are quartzite but the majority are largely of Torridonian sandstone, which provides the best routes. On the western edge of the area the latter forms the huge tiered cliffs of Beinn Bhan and Sgurr a' Chaorachain – famous for their winter climbs and the classic rock climbs of Cioch Nose (Very Difficult) and Sword of Gideon (VS). Further east are the Ben Damph and Coulin Forests, whose rocky peaks rise steeply from wild lochans. These are threaded by a good network of stalkers' paths, making it easy to link several scrambles on different hills into a lengthy scrambling day.

SGURR DUBH

782m   OS Landranger 25   (NG 979 558)

This predominantly quartzite hill dominates the south side of Glen Torridon. Although extremely rocky it doesn't run to continuous scrambles, the best being the prominent slabs above the Ling Hut.

91 North-West Slabs   Grade 3

Alt 300m   North-West facing   (NG 964 553)   Map p180   Diagram p182

These are quite technical in places, but non-serious, escapable virtually anywhere. The strata slope inwards, giving positive holds, but the fine-grained quartzite is very slippery in the wet.

Approach

Follow the path starting just east of the Coire Dubh car park (NG 958 569) past the Ling Hut up to around 200m, then slant up left to the prominent slabs. The lower left-hand tier has two slabby areas separated by a zone of small overhangs. Start below the right-hand slabby area at a separate slab about 30m lower, right of a scree patch. This is the lowest slab on the face.

The Route

Climb the slab, then a higher slab guarded by a small overlap. Go up left and climb a larger but more broken tier, then two more small slabs to reach the main cliff. Climb shattered slabs below and left of a large cracked pillar. Continue up smoother slabs by the delicate central crack to reach easy ground.

Ahead is a gorge, with cleaner steeper slabs up to the right. Go up to the left end of these, just left of the first vertical section. Gain a niche and exit up steep flakes on the right wall, then bear left up a slabby rib. More slabs lead past a sandstone boulder to the top.

Higher up there are sandstone slabs at NG 971 550, above two small

SGURR DUBH

91. North-West Slabs   Grade 3

lochans, then several more outcrops of both sandstone and quartzite can be found between here and the summit. Sgurr Dubh has many more outcrops with scrambling possibilities, notably the sandstone ribs below the minor summit at NG 976 559, the south-east facing sandstone slabs above Coire an Leth-uillt and the more serious quartzite slabs around NG 972 564.

BEINN LIATH MHOR

926m OS Landranger 25 (NG 964 519)

This is a steep-sided east-west ridge with three summits. Most of the rocky flanks are very broken, the only continuous rock being on the south flank of the East Summit. There are several larger buttresses to the left of the described route, but they have sections that are much more than scrambling.

92 South-East Rib   Grade 3   *

Alt 500m   South facing   (NG 987 509)   Map p180   Diagram p184

Short, but on excellent clean rock, providing an enjoyable alternative to the steepest part of the path.

Approach

From Achnashellach go up to the station, cross the line and follow the forestry road up right. Take the first fork left, then after half a kilometre a smaller path is signed off left. Follow this up alongside the river into Coire Lair. At the junction at NG 990 502 go straight ahead for about 400 metres, then head up right to the lowest buttress at the right-hand end of the cliff. Start on the left-hand side of this at a steep clean nose.

The Route

Climb the left-hand edge of the nose, which is very steep, but with good holds (some hidden round the left arête). Another steepening is climbed right of the arête, then rocky slopes lead up to a scree patch. Climb a steep wall by a square-cut groove right of centre, quite awkward at the top. Easy rock now leads up to grassy slopes, then a few more outcrops can be incorporated before the angle eases. The path at this point is well off to the right.

FUAR THOLL

907m   OS Landranger 25   (NG 975 489)

A fine peak, whose complex flanks provide a host of possibilities for scrambles, many more than those described.

93 South Flank   Grade 1 or 3   *

Alt 450m   South-East facing   (NG 984 484)   Map p180   Diagram p186

The face above Sgurr a' Mhuilinn is a huge sweep of sandstone slabs. The rock is excellent, although much of it is fairly easy-angled.

BEINN LIATH MHOR

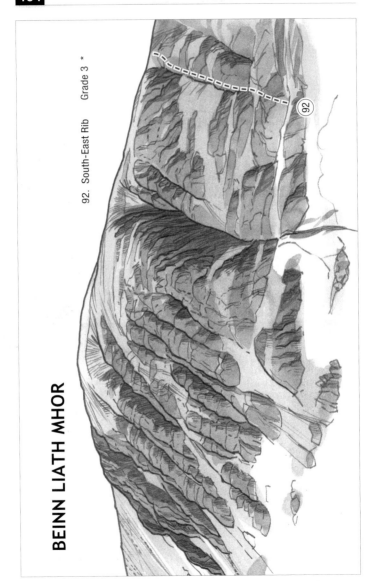

92. South-East Rib   Grade 3   *

92

*Lucy Williams on the right-hand slabs (Grade 2/3), south-east corrie, Fuar Tholl
Photo: Noel Williams*

FUAR THOLL

93a. South Flank   Grade 1 or 3 *

Approach
Start as for route 92 but once above the forestry go left and cross the River Lair. This can be difficult or even impossible in spate, the only bridge being the one for the railway at Achnashellach station. Follow a smaller stream up to the plateau of Sgurr a' Mhuillin at around 400m. The three widely-spaced lines described all lead to the summit of Fuar Tholl.

The Route(s)
a) The best route of the three follows the left-hand rim of the Fuar Tholl's south-eastern corrie – see the diagram on p186. Go up easy slabs by their right-hand edge, then smoother slabs offset to the right until these curve over to walking. A little higher two steeper ribs off right are worthwhile, then more slabby walking follows. A steeper band crosses the ridge above – easy direct, or Grade 3 by a vertical wall of spikes to the right. Boulders lead to another steep wall, climbed by a groove at its highest point. An easy slab and two short walls lead to easy ground.
b) The slabs below the right-hand edge of the main corrie also give a good scramble (Grade 2/3). Start at the lowest slab and climb directly to a prominent circular depression. Carry on up delightful slabs until they ease to walking. Higher up a pleasant narrow ridge leads leftwards to the summit.
c) 500 metres left of the first route a prominent clean rib gives easy scrambling with a steep wall at the top, climbed by a left to right ramp (Grade 1).

94 Spare Rib Moderate
Alt 550m North-East facing (NG 976 494) Map p180 Diagram p188
Steep in places and quite loose, with a precarious crux, but a good line with an excellent ridge to finish.

Approach
From Achnashellach follow the path up into Coire Lair as for Route 92, but turn left at NG 990 502. Follow the path up to the 550m contour, then traverse left to the cliff. This is split by three deep gullies, dividing it into four buttresses. The left-hand one is The Pile (Difficult, with a steep tower at half height). Spare Rib is the next right.

The Route
Start up small outcrops on the right-hand side of the buttress, just left of the gully. These get more sustained, then steepen considerably. Take grass ledges leading left, then go back up right to make a precarious mantelshelf into a niche left of the nose. Climb steeply out of this, hard and exposed. The worst is now over.

Go up vegetated steps left of the gully, then up the easy crest on loose blocks. Climb the next steepening by a tricky groove in the centre, then move right and climb a cleaner groove on the crest, finishing up big spikes. Start the next step on the right, then climb a crampon-scratched groove left of the crest. Finish up the spiky crest, to reach easier loose blocks. Traversing up and right leads into the north-west corrie below the next route.

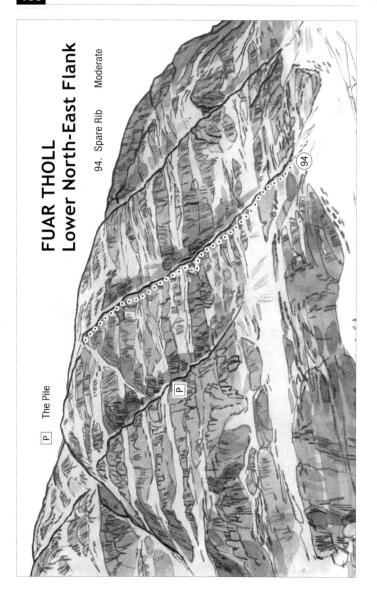

FUAR THOLL
Lower North-East Flank

94. Spare Rib   Moderate

P   The Pile

P

94

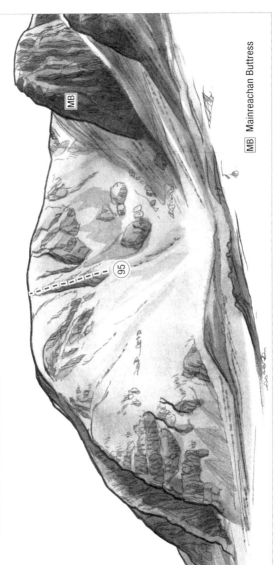

FUAR THOLL
North-West Flank

95. Summit Rib   Grade 3 *

MB Mainreachan Buttress

95 Summit Rib　Grade 3　*

Alt 800m　North-West facing　(NG 975 490)　Map p180　Diagram p189

Short but excellent scrambling in good positions.

Approach

This is the middle of the three buttresses just under the summit on its north-west side. It can be reached easily from below, up the north-west corrie, or by traversing north-eastwards from the col between the impressively steep Mainreachan Buttress (NG 972 489) and the main summit. The rib has an open easy gully to its right and a deep cut narrower one to its left. Start at the lowest point.

The Route

Go up a juggy rib, then a steep quartz slab on small sharp edges. Swing right-to-left up a vertical wall, then follow more juggy steps on the left edge (quite loose). The angle eases off, with a steep flake crack off to the right giving a hard variation. Higher up a juggy prow leads to a narrow arête, then easy ground goes up to the summit.

SGORR RUADH

962m　OS Landranger 25　(NG 959 505)

The highest peak of the Coulin Forest throws down two huge buttresses into Coire Lair to the north-east. Most of this is very steep, but variants of the two classic rock climbs make good scrambles.

96 Academy Ridge, Lower Slabs　Grade 3

Alt 500m　North-East facing　(NG 970 507)　Map p180　Diagram p191

The lower part of this Very Difficult climb is mostly easy slabs, with a couple of short awkward sections. It makes a good prelude to Raeburn's Buttress.

Approach

From Achnashellach take the track up Coire Lair as for Route 92, but continue ahead until beyond the loch. The two buttresses up on the left are Academy Ridge on the left and Raeburn's Buttress on the right. Start at the bottom right-hand corner of the former, right of a vertical wall with slabs above.

The Route

Climb the right-hand arête until forced right below blanker rock. Go back up left as soon as possible to a nose. Keep moving up left until a flake crack allows access to the arête. Follow the skyline, with plenty of scope for variation, until it eases to walking. The top part of Academy Ridge is a serious Very Difficult, so traverse off right into a shallow corrie (escapes both upwards and downwards). Continuing further right below steep cliffs reaches the next route.

SGORR RUADH

96. Academy Ridge, Lower Slabs   Grade 3
97. Raeburn's Buttress   Grade 3 **

97 Raeburn's Buttress   Grade 3   **

Alt 600m   North-East facing   (NG 966 509)   Map p180   Diagram p191

This is the right-hand of Sgorr Ruadh's two buttresses as seen from Coire Lair. Avoiding the Difficult start to the original route provides excellent juggy scrambling, quite steep and exposed in places, but with good holds and friction.

Approach

Either approach direct from Coire Lair up the shallow corrie between the two buttresses or traverse right after the previous route. On the right-hand side of the shallow corrie is a narrow gully just left of the skyline. Start here.

The Route

The original route starts up steep rock right of the gully and is Difficult, so climb the gully until above the chockstone. Bear up right to a stony shelf and follow this right to the skyline. Climb the steep central nose (some loose holds) to a pinnacle. Climb the right-hand of two ribs to a ledge, then make an awkward step up left into a mossy groove. Carry on up this and its right-hand arête. Where this fades go up left to the skyline and continue up this, with the odd problem. A short walk then takes you to the sting in the tail. The ridge narrows and bears right. Climb the first tower starting on the left and bearing up right to take the nose direct. Climb a second nose direct, then a third larger nose direct too. This last looks highly unlikely, but good holds make the exposure bearable. Walking leads to the north-east summit.

AN RUADH-STAC

892m   OS Landranger 25   (NG 921 480)

An excellent peak that just fails to reach Munro height. The quartzite slabs on the east flank provide good scrambling, and the Allt Moin' a' Chriathair makes an entertaining approach.

98 Allt Moin' a' Chriathair   Grade 2 or 3   *

Alt 100m   South-East facing   (NG 951 465)   Map p180

First a bouldery gorge, then better and more open scrambling up steep steps beside scenic falls. The route is escapable in numerous places, while the better upper part can easily be done on its own.

Approach

Usually it is easy to cross the main Fionn Abhainn at the mouth of the Allt Moin' a' Chriathair (and if it isn't then you shouldn't be doing this route!). There is a bridge 600 metres upstream.

The Route

An easy gorge leads to the first fall, climbed on the right with a hard pull-up to start. Follow a central rib to more boulders. Climb the next fall on the right, followed by a very slippery shelf. A large boulder (avoidable on the

AN RUADH-STAC

99. Eastern Slabs   Grade 2 or Moderate **

left) leads to an easy section. Leaning walls then force you out of the gorge. Return briefly for an easy bit, then two more falls need avoiding. Return as the gorge opens out, where pretty slabs and a couple of small falls lead to a long level open section.

Enter the next gorge by a delicate move to a slippery shelf on the left, then cross and go along a ledge past a holly. Climb the next fall either by a jump on the left (slippery landing) or a precarious shelf on the right. Pass the next fall by a chimney on the right to reach an easy section, terminated by a big fall coming in on the left.

The character now changes to steeper and more open falls, and the route can easily be started here to take in just the best scrambling (Grade 2). Climb juggy walls right of the stream to a long shelf. Halfway along this cross and climb the wall on the left on good holds to another shelf. At the far end of this climb cracked boulders and a short wall to more slabs and the finish. A short walk leads up past a lochan to the next route.

 99 Eastern Slabs   Grade 2 or Moderate   **
Alt 500m   East facing   (NG 928 481)   Map p180   Diagram p193
Open quartzite slabs, delicate in places.

Approach
From the lowest point of the saddle east of An Ruadh-stac traverse south-west below easy slabs to the second smooth slab, directly above the largest lochan.

The Route
Climb the easy slab, then walk up broken ground to go up another smooth slab with a vertical right-hand wall. Where this reaches steeper steps go left along a ledge below steeper rock into the central bay. Direct routes from here are delicate and around Moderate, but the best line is to carry on along the ledge until below a slabby corner with a vertical left-hand wall. Tiptoe delicately up the corner in a superb position. At the top climb the first overlap by stepping in from the right, then climb the second overlap direct to easy ground. Near the top of the ridge a short detour right leads to small buttresses which give a pleasant Grade 2 finish.

MAOL CHEAN-DEARG

933m   OS Landranger 25   (NG 924 499)

A fairly easy Munro when approached from the south-east, while the north side of the hill is steep, wild and little frequented.

 100 Ketchil Buttress   Grade 3 or Difficult   *
Alt 600m   East facing   (NG 931 492)   Map p180
Steep quartzite steps on good square-cut holds. An enjoyable alternative to the steep scree-ridden section on the usual path.

Noel Williams on Ketchil Buttress (Grade3), Maol Chean-dearg
Photo: Iain Thow

MAOL CHEAN-DEARG

101. North Flank   Grade 1/2

Approach
From Coulags in Strath Carron (NG 958 451) follow the path northwards up the Fionn Abhainn. 1km beyond the bothy fork left and follow the zigzag path as far as the 500m contour. Now head up right to a quartzite face. The left-hand side of this is a long line of cliffs low down, while the right-hand side has two bigger buttresses at a higher level. Ketchil Buttress is the left-hand one. Start at twin ribs separated by an alcove. The right-hand buttress is a similar grade, but looser and a poorer line.

The Route
Climb the left-hand rib (the right-hand one is a loose and awkward Difficult). Climb another step above, then a steeper step using flakes just right of the nose. Easier rock then leads up to a final steep wall, which can either be tackled direct (Difficult) or dodged by a ramp on the right.

101 North Flank   Grade 1/2
Alt 600m   North facing   (NG 929 501)   Map p180   Diagram p196

Mainly steep walking, but the final ridge is good and the setting wild and impressive. A harder alternative is the steep buttress forming the left edge of the face – easier than it looks (Grade 2). Start left of centre then work rightwards up grassy rakes until feasible routes appear through the steeper tiers.

Approach
From Annat on Loch Torridon (NG 894 544) take the signed footpath running up south-east from the shore road about 100 metres west of the phone box, starting in a small wood. Follow this to Loch an Eoin, then fork left to the Bealach na Lice (NG 933 509). Go up southwards past boulder problems and follow the shoulder up until it runs into the main hill. Ahead is a large bay with a steep cliff on its left and a ramp leading up right. This becomes a gully higher up (Hidden Gully). The route follows the right edge of this.

The Route
Start up a broken buttress on the right of the main bay. This is steep to start, then gradually eases to walking. Walk rightwards up the ramp, with a few outcrops, then when the gully becomes more defined cross to the right bank. A series of short steps are tackled direct, then a fun knife edge. The next vertical step is climbed by a groove on the right, then a few more steps lead to easy ground just below the summit.

896m   OS Landranger 24   (NG 804 450)

The highest of the Applecross hills, with a magnificent line of corries on its north-east flank. The three finest are (left to right) Coire na Feola, Coire na Poite and Coire nan Fhamhair and these are separated by the prominent ridges of A' Chioch (Moderate) on the left and A' Phoit (Severe) on the right.

COULIN & APPLECROSS

Iain Thow on A' Chioch (Moderate), Beinn Bhan
Photo: Noel Williams

102 A' Chioch   Moderate   **

Alt 450m   East facing   (NG 819 446)   Map p180

Rather patchy scrambling, but a good line with awesome situations. Exposed, with some vegetation and a few loose blocks.

Approach
From the bridge over the River Kishorn at Tornapress (NG 834 423) take the path running up northwards. Leave it after about 2km to follow the stream up into Coire na Feola. A' Chioch is the right-hand arête.

The Route
The ridge starts as a broad buttress, where a steep bouldery start leads to broken rocks. Cleaner slabs to the left give a good harder variation. Once over the first crest more bouldery walking leads to a row of stepped ribs on the right. The left-hand one is excellent, finishing up a flake crack. The ridge now narrows before another steepening. Vertical rocks on the right can be climbed on their left edge on good holds or avoided on the left. Broken tiers lead to the top of A' Chioch.

Descend a narrow ridge to grass, then an awkward steep descent leads to a notch. An easier variation descends a gully on the left and an exposed grassy ramp. From the notch either climb the steep rib of blocks ahead or use the gully on the left to reach the next top. Descend on the right, then take a narrow ledge left to a notch. More direct descents are steep and loose. Pass left of the pinnacles to reach the very steep headwall. A well-used route climbs this just right of the arête, quite vegetated, until the ground opens out below a steeper tier. Climb the awkward gully in the centre using a handy jammed block, then go up and left to more open slabs and a final easy ridge. The summit is a few hundred metres to the right.

SGURR A' CHAORACHAIN

792m   OS Landranger 24   (NG 796 417)

Very impressive from a distance, this sandstone dome dominates Loch Kishorn, and some good rock climbs are found along its sides, including the classics Cioch Nose (Very Difficult) and Sword of Gideon (VS).

103 Cioch Indirect   Difficult   **

Alt 400m   South-East facing   (NG 796 426)   Map p180   Diagram p200
A major expedition, exposed in places and technical in others. The line is not always obvious and, although big ledges often mitigate the exposure, the situations are impressive and the positions serious.

Approach
Park at the bridge over the Russel Burn and from the next bend take a boggy track to Loch Coire nan Arr. From the far end of this slant up north-west into the mouth of Coire a' Chaorachain, with the Cioch looming ahead. Start below South Gully, the major gully left of the Cioch, just left of a scree patch.

The Route
Climb two short outcrops to the mouth of South Gully. Go up easy rocks just right of the gully, then either traverse into it and climb it damply to a steep

SGURR A' CHAORACHAIN

103. Cioch Indirect   Difficult **

wall, or climb the left-hand edge of a chimney just to the right (steep), then traverse into the gully below the steep wall.

Go left into a subsidiary gully (Anonymous Gully), up this for 10m, then right again to rejoin South Gully. Climb the gully, with a short hard pitch (usually wet). The col behind the Cioch is now easy to reach, but more fun is to walk right along a terrace to the arête and climb this on big flakes and blocks to the top of the Cioch.

Beyond the col dodge the first step on the left (path) and continue up the ridge. This steepens, with an airy step right near the top, before reaching a good ledge below a large vertical wall. Follow the ledge left across Anonymous Gully and out to the arête. Just beyond this climb a steep open groove slanting left, just left of a pile of blocks. At its top step left and go up a short wet gully, then right along a ledge to the skyline. Climb this airily on big rough flakes. Now follow the ridge over a series of towers, with some easy scrambling up them. The first, third and fifth towers have steep awkward descents.

A good continuation is to carry on round to the main top of Sgurr a' Chaorachain and descend the south-east shoulder, which is steep, with occasional short bits of scrambling and great views.

MEALL GORM

710m   OS Landranger 24   (NG 778 409)

The terraced cliffs rimming the southern flank of the Bealach na Ba feature in many a photograph. Most of the buttresses are too steep for scrambling, but there are exceptions. The broken buttress left of the narrow Blue Pillar (Very Difficult) near the right-hand end of the cliff has a nice finish, but the route described below is better.

104 Long Buttress   Grade 2
Alt 400m   North facing   (NG 788 408)   Map p180   Diagram p202

This is the long stepped buttress running down to the step in the corrie floor. Generally follow the right-hand edge, up short steep walls with a wide choice of route.

Approach
Halfway up the Bealach na Ba road there is a small parking place on the right just above the step in the corrie floor. Cross the corrie to a small outcrop with a large perched block at half height.

The Route
Climb the right-hand edges of the first two outcrops. The next outcrop is steep, so climb a rib right of a grassy rake. More short buttresses follow, with many possible lines, a small detached pinnacle and a flaky prow being worthwhile. Bear left up short walls to finish up an excellent slabby wall. Harder variations are possible taking the larger buttresses direct.

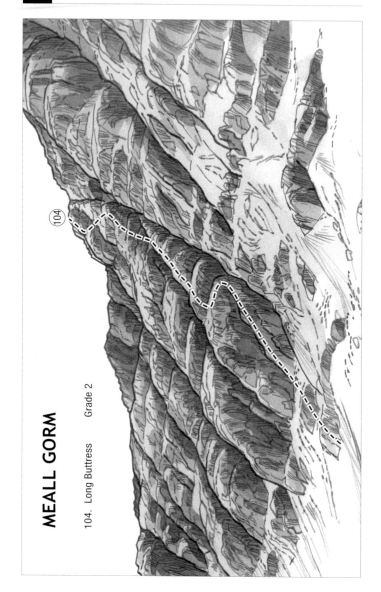

MEALL GORM

104. Long Buttress   Grade 2

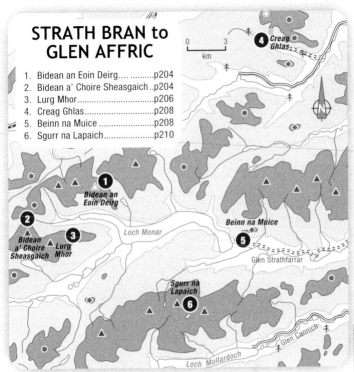

STRATH BRAN to GLEN AFFRIC

0   3
km

Creag Ghlas

Bidean an Eoin Deirg

Loch Monar

Bidean a' Choire Sheasgaich

Lurg Mhor

Beinn na Muice

Glen Strathfarrar

Sgurr na Lapaich

Glen Cannich

Loch Mullardoch

STRATH BRAN TO GLEN AFFRIC

This area is a peak-baggers' paradise, with summits spread out along sweeping ridges running west to east, separated by broad deep glens. The north-western hills are usually accessed from Glen Carron and form a more compact knot. Distances are long here, but the good estate track up the Allt a' Chonais makes the approach easy (a mountain bike is useful). The other hills rise above Strath Conon, Glen Strathfarrar, Glen Cannich and Glen Affric and are easily reached from the east.

Although this area is not one of the rockier parts of the North-West, there are still good scrambles to be had. Most of them are on the ridges linking the major peaks of the area and fall into the category of incidents in a mountain day spent traversing a number of hills rather than being objectives in themselves. A pleasant contrast with most of the North-West is that the glens carry a fair amount of woodland, both commercial forestry and size-able areas of ancient forest. The Scots Pines of Glens Affric and Strathfarrar in particular are outstanding, and add greatly to the pleasures of a day here. The road up Glen Strathfarrar is private, with a locked gate just above Struy. At present access is allowed between 9am and 7pm, except all day on Tuesdays and on Wednesday mornings.

BIDEAN AN EOIN DEIRG

1046m   OS Landranger 25   (NH 103 443)

This subsidiary top of the sprawling Sgurr a' Chaorachain has a nice pointed summit and a steep, sharp north-east ridge.

105 North-East Ridge   Grade 1 or 2
Alt 800m   North-East facing   (NH 105 445)   Map p203

A bouldery spur, but with a few short outcrops. If the first two slabs are avoided the route is only Grade 1.

Approach
From Craig (NH 040 493) take the forestry road up the Allt a' Chonais until just short of Glenuaig Lodge. Head south-east up grassy slopes into the valley of An Crom Allt and follow this up to the saddle below the west ridge of Carn nam Fiaclan. Traverse south-east below some steep slabs, then head up to a prominent pink slab at the foot of the main spur.

The Route
Climb the pink slab, then traverse left past a smaller ridge to another slab. Go up the left arête of this. Easier slabs then lead to a broad spur, mainly grassy. As the ridge narrows more easy slabs can be included, then short out-crops alternate with boulders. The spur narrows and steepens, still mainly boulders, but with a few small outcrops. At the top a steeper rib and mossy boulders lead directly to the cairn.

BIDEIN A' CHOIRE SHEASGAICH

945m   OS Landranger 25   (NH 049 412)

A remote Munro with a lot of rather vegetated crags, including the 100m high North Face which falls in two steep tiers to the Bealach an Sgoltaidh. It is almost always combined with Lurg Mhor on the basis that once you've done the enormous walk in for one you might as well climb both.

106 North Face   Grade 3
Alt 650m   North facing   (NH 048 422)   Map p203   Diagram p205

A scramble in two disjointed halves, a lower tier of steep but positive slabs,

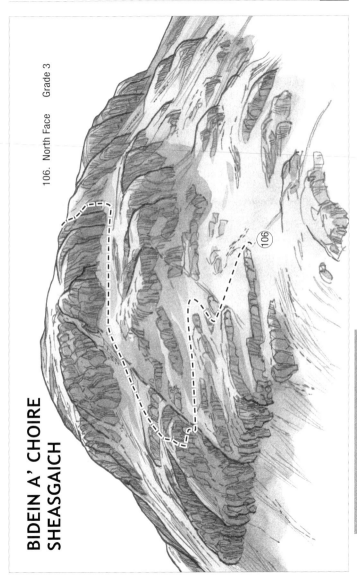

BIDEIN A' CHOIRE
SHEASGAICH

106. North Face   Grade 3

(106)

and a more serious upper tier of juggier but looser rock. Basically a way of adding interest to a steep path.

Approach
The usual approach is from Craig (NH 040 493), taking the vehicle track to NH 074 468 then crossing the river (single wire but no bridge) to go up to the Bealach Bhearnais. Either climb Beinn Tharsuinn or traverse across its south-east shoulder, then descend to the Bealach an Sgoltaidh. On the crest of the pass is a wall. From the south end of this follow a steep path zigzagging up left. Pass right of a steep slab, then above it walk 100 metres left to a larger clean slab. Start at the bottom right-hand corner of this.

The Route
Delicate moves lead up the edge to a ledge at 5m. Follow this left across the slab until just before the left-hand edge. This point can easily be reached direct, but with less fun. Go up on good holds, moving right near the top to avoid a dirtier section. Go up minor outcrops and grass to another slab and climb it just right of the left-hand edge on good holds. Follow a large terrace up right to meet the path below a steep grassy gully.

The path exits up this, but if in search of more excitement walk a long way right below the upper tier until the steep cliffs above begin to break up into shattered ribs. Take the first rib right of the overhangs, quite broken and mossy at first, but cleaner and juggy above (some loose holds). The rib ends on steep grass with a mossy slab above and overhangs to the left. Go up left and cross the top of a minor gully to get onto the next rib above the overhangs. Climb this airily on big holds. Another exposed rib then leads to the top of the crag. A few boulder problems can be found further up the ridge, notably two superb rippled slabs just before and after the largest lochan.

LURG MHOR

986m   OS Landranger 25   (NH 064 404)

A very remote Munro perched above the head of Loch Monar. The ridge between the two tops has a short section of unavoidable scrambling.

107 Meall Mor Ridge   Grade 1
Alt 950m   (NH 067 404)   Map p203

A couple of awkward steps on a narrow ridge.

Approach
Lurg Mhor is a very long way from anywhere. It is most commonly approached by climbing Bidean a' Choire Sheasgaich first (as for Route 106). Descend south-east to a saddle and climb broad slopes to Lurg Mhor.

The Route
From the summit follow the ridge eastwards and descend a sharp slabby crest (path to the right). Make an exposed step down, then descend another sharp crest to a saddle. Go up steeply to a minor summit, then pass airily left

CREAG GHLAS

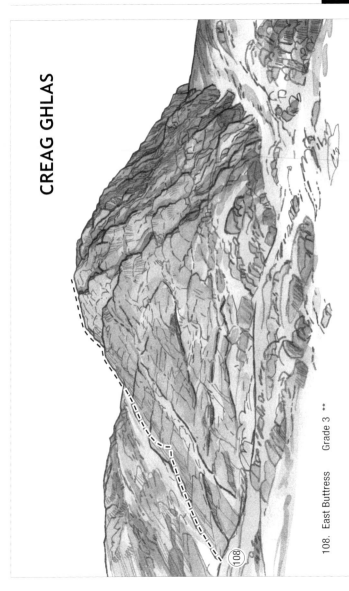

108. East Buttress   Grade 3 **

of a small tower to a notch. Go up the far side on big flakes, then an easy narrow ridge leads to the rounded top of Meall Mor.

CREAG GHLAS

686m   OS Landranger 25   (NH 246 547)

This subsidiary top of the Strathconon Corbett Sgurr a' Mhuilinn has a large south-west face consisting of two buttresses of steep schistose grit. The larger East Buttress is 250m high and broken into a series of slabby tiers. A good way to start a loop around the two Corbetts.

108 East Buttress   Grade 3   **
Alt 350m   South-West facing   (NH 246 544)   Map p203   Diagram p207
The left-hand edge is taken by the broken rock climb Oh Dear – given the strange (but accurate!) grade of Difficult to VS. This makes an excellent scramble if the harder parts are avoided. Climbers may prefer to take rock boots and tackle these more directly, giving an extended series of boulder problems.

Approach
Take the forestry track up Gleann Meinich to NH 244 541, then turn right up a break in the forest. Once above the trees slant up right to the base of the cliff. Start at the left-hand end of the main slab, just right of a narrow gully.

The Route
There are various cracks on the slab at Severe to VS, but scramblers should start by a vegetated groove on the left, stepping right onto the slab as the angle eases. Go up a right-slanting groove until a step left leads to a ledge and the top of the tier. Follow easy slabs (best on the left) to a steeper tier. Go down right to climb steps leading back up left (awkward), then go left to the edge and up. Avoid the next slab by a grassy groove on the right (delicate Very Difficult direct). A broken groove leads up the next tier (or thin cracks near the left edge, Difficult). The slabs now ease until a short vertical wall is bypassed to reach a larger wall. A broken groove on the left leads to a cleaner finish (the steep square-cut corner on the right leads to a juggy finish at Very Difficult). Numerous slabby boulder problems now lead to the east summit. From the saddle on the left clean easy-angled ribs lead to the higher west summit.

BEINN NA MUICE

693m   OS Landranger 25   (NH 218 402)

This isolated rocky hill rises steeply above the Monar Dam, giving superb views.

BEINN NA MUICE

109. South-West Slabs   Grade 2 or 3

109 South-West Slabs   Grade 2 or 3
Alt 350m   South facing   (NH 209 399)   Map p203   Diagram p209

The hillside is scattered with slabs of excellent knobbly schistose grit, varying from walking angle to 50 degrees, becoming more sustained and steeper towards the top. There is a huge choice of route.

Approach

Park 0.5km before the Monar Dam, where a rough vehicle track goes off northwards. In a few hundred metres this stops at a dump. Head north-west up the hillside to the first slabs. At the top are two larger masses of rock, and the best route links together slabs up leftwards towards the left-hand one.

The Route

The first slabs start at walking angle, then steepen before running out into heather. Bear up left, taking in the cleanest slabs. These can be quite smooth, but are scattered with knobbly holds. As with most slabs, small changes in angle make a big difference. Arrive on the ridge just below and left of the left-hand steeper buttress.

There are a few outcrops on the ridge itself, but it is better to traverse right and zigzag up the steeper buttress (the direct is harder than it looks, Grade 3). From its top another traverse right allows the inclusion of the right-hand buttress, which consists of excellent Grade 2 slabs. A pleasant ridge then leads to the summit. The eastern summit is higher, but the western one has the better view.

SGURR NA LAPAICH

1150m   OS Landranger 25   (NH 160 351)

One of the dominant peaks of the area, this has a pointed summit and several good ridges, although only one of these runs to scrambling.

110 East Ridge   Grade 1
Alt 900m   East facing   (NH 167 351)   Map p203

A bouldery ridge, narrow in places.

Approach

Although it can be approached directly from the power station in Gleann Innis an Loichel (short but steep and rough) the ridge is most often climbed during a traverse of the Mullardoch Munros. From the saddle between Carn nan Gobhar and Sgurr na Lapaich start up a gentle ridge, then go right to join the rocky crest at a large square-cut boulder.

The Route

Climb onto the boulder from the left, step right across a gap, then go left and through a flaky gap in a steep face. Boulders and moss lead up to a grassy ridge, then move right onto a slabby crest. Avoid a steeper slab, or climb it by a grassy crack and quartz nodules at Grade 3. As the ridge narrows keep to the crest for the most fun and cross a minor summit. A clamber up large boulders leads to the main summit.

CARN EIGE

1183m   OS Landranger 25   (NH 123 261)

The highest summits north of the Great Glen, Carn Eige and its twin summit Mam Sodhail are the focal points of a sprawl of ridges between Glen Affric and Loch Mullardoch. Most of these are grassy, but the east ridge breaks into a row of shattered pinnacles about 1.5km from the summit.

 111 Carn Eige Pinnacles   Grade 1
Alt 1100m   (NH 137 263)   Map p212

A sharp spiky ridge, avoidable on its south flank.

Approach
The pinnacles are usually traversed from east to west while en route from Tom a' Choinich to Carn Eige. After the steep rise to Sron Garbh (NH 145 264, unnamed on the OS 1:50,000 map), pass over the minor top of Stob Coire Dhomhnuill (NH 139 262, also unnamed on the 1:50,000 map) to reach the sharp ridge.

The Route
A narrow ridge and an easy blocky pinnacle lead to a broad saddle, then go up steep spikes to cross the first pinnacle. Climb a bigger pinnacle easily, descending leftwards just before the top. Go up the second large pinnacle, dodging its summit on the right to reach a steep juggy descent. Blocks lead up to Stob a' Choire Dhomhain and the end of the difficulties.

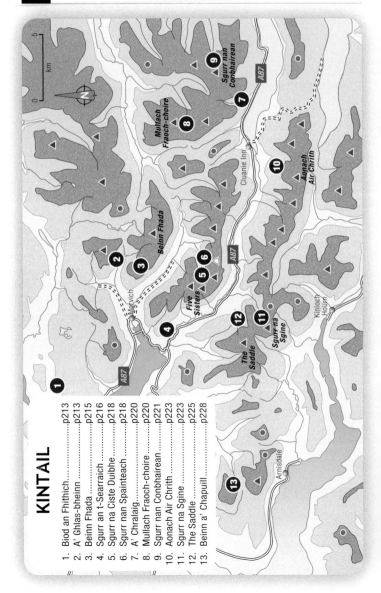

KINTAIL

Sgurr nan Conbhairean

A87

Mullach Fraoch-choire

Cluanie Inn

Aonach Air Chrith

Beinn Fhada

A87

Five Sisters

Morvich

Kinloch Hourn

Sgurr na Sgine

The Saddle

A87

Arnisdale

km

KINTAIL

The two ridges either side of the massive through valley of Glenshiel/Cluanie are a paradise for ridge wanderers. Although the main ridges themselves are easy, several side ridges provide good scrambles, with the Forcan Ridge of the Saddle being a classic. These are schist hills, so some of these routes are a bit vegetated and/or discontinuous, but they are still worthwhile, especially as a prelude to a leisurely wander along the Cluanie Ridge or the Five Sisters. Closer to the coast more isolated hills such as A' Ghlas Bheinn or Beinn a' Chapuill can also provide entertainment, with the stream scramble on the former being the longest (and probably wettest) route in this guide.

BIOD AN FHITHICH

330m OS Landranger 33 (NG 916 273)

A rather vegetated north-facing crag with a clean slabby right-hand side overlooking the River Glennan in the wild land north of Dornie.

112 Ankle Ridge Difficult *
Alt 150m North facing (NG 914 275) Map 212 Diagram p214

Slabby quartzite ribs scattered with incut holds. Easy for the grade with lots of possible variations. A good evening route.

Approach

From Bundalloch on the east side of Loch Long take the path up the River Glennan for 1.5km. Cross the river and slog up heather to the right-hand edge of the lowest buttress.

The Route

Climb the right-hand edge of the buttress on positive holds to a heather terrace below the main crag. From the highest point of the terrace climb orange rock moving right. Make an awkward step right onto a rib and go up its right-hand edge to the edge of the crag. Go up the arête (easy-angled but quite delicate). Where this is split by a heathery groove the left-hand rib is better. An overhanging nose can be climbed on its right or avoided on its left to reach a large niche. Go left to the obvious rib and follow it to the top.

There is good bouldering just beyond the top. Descend well to the left (looking out), as the gullies either side are unpleasant.

A' GHLAS-BHEINN

918m OS Landranger 33 (NG 008 230)

This knobbly Munro blocks the end of Strath Croe, with several prominent gullies running down its south-west slopes. These have some scrappy scrambling low down, but the hidden stream running down further east into Gleann Choinneachain is much better.

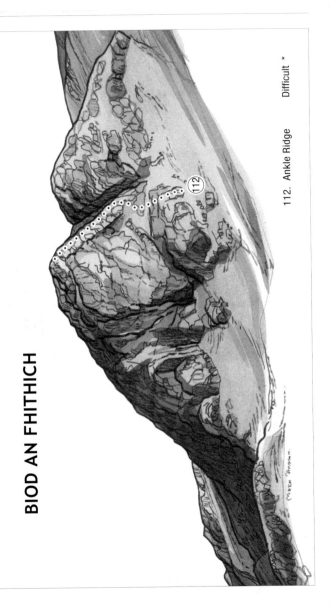

BIOD AN FHITHICH

112. Ankle Ridge   Difficult *

113 Allt Loch a' Chleirich Moderate **

Alt 150m   South-West facing   (NG 997 220)   Map p212

A very long and sustained stream scramble, with almost all falls climbable, albeit in the stream at times. Save it for a dry spell and still be prepared to get very wet!

Approach

From Dorusdain (NG 981 224) follow the forestry track up through the woods on the north side of Gleann Choinneachain, keeping to the lowest forks. Where this turns sharply back left go straight on, still on a good track, to emerge from the forest at a bridge.

The Route

Climb the first fall by traversing in from the right above the pool. Three more falls follow, taken on the right, left and right respectively to reach the end of the first gorge. A large fall now comes in on the left. Start this on the right, cross at the initial pool, then start up a clean rib on the left. This gets harder and forces you off right into a grassy groove. Gain a grass ramp further right awkwardly and follow it to the top of the rib.

Regain the stream above the big fall and cross its top (easy but exposed). Go up a central rib, then cross the stream leftwards again to climb a short steep wall on sharp holds. Cross slabs rightwards and go up a runnel left of the main flow. Cross again twice in quick succession and go up easily to a gorge. Although initially looking promising, this has a horrendously slimy exit, so is better avoided on the right. Descend into the stream above the next falls, climb a clean rib on the far bank, then follow the left edge. The next gorge starts easily, then at the first fall pull up onto a shelf on the left, traverse along it and climb a niche left of the fall. The next fall is passed by a technical traverse low on the right wall, and the next by going up right of the fall. Exit the gorge on the right and rejoin the stream above.

Climb a fall in the flow and avoid the next by starting up a small side stream on the right, then traversing back in across steep grass. Climb another fall on the left on small holds, then the stream forks. Take the right branch. After one fall and an easy section a more serious obstacle is passed by a traverse across the wall on the right on loose spikes. Easy little falls follow, then the last big fall is avoided by a grassy gully on the left. Another easy section leads to a succession of small falls, one climbed in the stream on sharp red holds. None are hard and most are avoidable as the gorge opens out before arriving at the lochan – 500m above the start.

BEINN FHADA

1032m   OS Landranger 33   (NH 018 192)

A long ridge running from Strath Croe to the head of Glen Affric with some easy scrambling on the north-west end. The slabby buttresses below this on the north impress from a distance but are horribly loose.

114 Bealach an t-Sealgaire (Hunters' Pass) **Grade 1**
Alt 850m *(NG 993 204)* *Map p212*

A broken ridge with one short harder step.

Approach

From the foot of Gleann Lichd (limited parking at NG 966 210) take the road crossing the river to Innis a' Chrotha. Follow the path until you can go up the grassy slopes ahead to a gate, then continue up Beinn Bhuidhe. The ridge curves rightwards as you gain height and becomes rockier over Sgurr a' Choire Ghairbh.

The Route

The first minor summits provide a few small outcrops to play on, but the best scrambling is on the descent to the notch of Hunters' Pass. Go down into a slabby groove, avoiding the steeper bottom section by a ramp on the left. A pleasant ridge leads over Ceum na h-Aon-choise and Meall an Fhuarain Mhoir before a stroll across the plateau to the main summit.

SGURR AN T-SEARRAICH

576m **OS Landranger 33** **(NG 950 191)**

This subsidiary summit of the Five Sisters is a superb viewpoint and has a series of slabby ribs running south from the summit, well seen from the Glen Shiel road. These make a good start to a traverse of the ridge or a short excursion in their own right.

 115 South Ribs **Grade 3**
Alt 50m *South facing* *(NG 946 184)* *Map 212* *Diagram p217*

A string of short schist outcrops with some hard moves but little exposure. Vegetation low down makes for hard going in summer.

Approach

From the Shiel Bridge shop cross the bridge and turn right along the river. Head up through bracken to reach a gate in the fence to the right. Follow a small path along to the reedy Loch Shiel. At a stone wall just before the far end of the loch go up past small clifflets to the lowest point of the main slabs.

The Route

Go up the slabs to a niche full of blackberries. Traverse right to a ledge, then go left up a heather ramp for a few feet. Climb the unlikely-looking wall on the right, which is full of nice surprises. Slabs and heather then lead to an easing. Walk up the spur via a couple of minor outcrops. At the top walk up left to reach the next outcrop above its main steeper cliff. Go up this to climb the right edge of slabs. Cross the next hump and go up to climb the left-hand end of the crag above. A juggy rib follows, then go right up a grassy ramp to climb a clean slab – quite hard.

SGURR AN T-SEARRAICH

115. South Ribs   Grade 3

More little outcrops can be included as you go up the spur. At its top go horizontally right to the next spur. Climb the front of this on jugs, then several more short steep outcrops. Where the spur runs out climb slabs on the right to another minor top. Climb the obvious clean slab ahead, then outcrops working up left, aiming for a larger crag on the skyline. Climb the groove in the centre of this, with a long step right onto a nose.

More outcrops follow, still heading up left, notably a left-sloping groove with a hard start and a steep juggy wall (avoiding the top overhang on the right). Finish up easy left-sloping slabs with a short walk to the summit.

SGURR NA CISTE DUIBHE

1027m   OS Landranger 33   (NG 984 149)

The rightmost of the Five Sisters in the popular view, with long rough slopes falling to Glenshiel and a hidden craggy north side.

116 North Buttress   Grade 1
Alt 700m   North facing   (NG 985 153)   Map p212   Diagram p219

A rocky ridge with only limited scrambling but good positions.

Approach
Either traverse from the Ciste Duibhe/Carnach col (easy), or use a steeper traverse from the strange offset saddle east of Sgurr na Ciste Duibhe. In the latter case slant down northwards from the west end of the saddle, keeping below slabs until it is easy to slant up to the ridge.

The Route
An easy ridge leads to boulders, then a narrowing leads to a notch. A short steeper section on good holds and more boulders lead to a minor top, then a short loose descent and walking takes you to the summit.

SGURR NAN SPAINTEACH

990m   OS Landranger 33   (NG 991 150)

This is the forgotten sixth Sister hidden away from the popular viewpoints but with a nice summit poised above Coire Dhomdain.

117 North Buttress   Grade 2
Alt 800m   North facing   (NG 994 153)   Map p212   Diagram p219

A blunt schist buttress with a wide choice of route and little exposure. Some technical moves, easily avoided.

Approach
Either descend grass slopes east of the summit to the foot of the buttress, or more scenically traverse in from the Bealach an Lapain at the east end of the Five Sisters ridge. There is a small path at first, rounding the initial spur, then

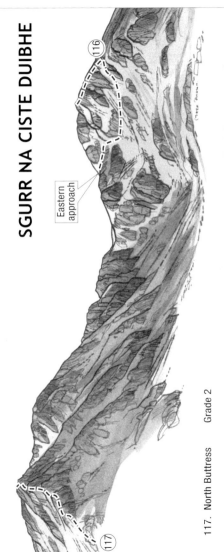

SGURR NAN SPAINTEACH

SGURR NA CISTE DUIBHE

Eastern approach

117. North Buttress   Grade 2

116. North Buttress   Grade 1

traverse to and across a small shelf before slanting down to the foot of the buttress, about 1.5km from the Bealach. Start at an ill-defined bouldery ridge down left from two triangular faces.

The Route
Follow the ridge until above the triangular faces, then traverse right to another triangular face above the others. Climb the right-hand edge of this. Follow a broken ridge until a traverse right leads to another triangular face, climbed from left to right (hard but avoidable). Go up blocks, then climb a short wall crossing the buttress, starting just left of a spike. Go up left to the skyline and follow it to boulders. A short steep section above a niche leads to more boulders and the top.

A' CHRALAIG

1120m   OS Landranger 34   (NH 094 148)

A big grassy mountain with nice ridges. The stream described provides an alternative approach to the usual slog up from Cluanie.

 118 Allt Choire a' Chait   Grade 2
Alt 250m   South facing   (NH 107 113)   Map p212

A long and scenic series of falls, not sustained and all avoidable. The schist slabs are beautifully patterned, but wickedly slippery when wet.

Approach
There are parking places a few hundred metres either side of the stream.

The Route
100m above the bridge the first gorge is climbed by pocketed slabs on the left. Just after large boulders in midstream go up patterned slabs on the left. At a narrowing stay on the left, close to the water at first, then up a gnarled slab. Keep on the left until an impassable pool forces you out. A few metres higher a horizontal ledge leads back in, followed by an awkward move up onto slabs on the left. At the top cross back right by a boulder. Avoid two pools, then drop back into the stream bed and climb two sets of beautifully patterned slabs. Keep right, avoiding one pool, until the bed opens out.

Go up the left bank to a larger fall, climbed by a quartzy wall well left of the water. Cross back right and go up a few steps to easy ground. At an upper fall take the right-hand branch, keeping right when it forks. Higher up another fall is climbed on the left by a delicate traverse and slabs, then another by more slabs. A couple of higher falls need to be avoided.

MULLACH FRAOCH-CHOIRE

1102m   OS Landranger 34   (NH 094 171)

A sharp top with three ridges, the southern one with some easy scrambling.

119 South Ridge   Grade 1 or 2   *
Alt 1000m   South facing   (NH 095 165)   Map p212

A series of pleasant pinnacles add interest to a narrow ridge. Difficulties can be sought or avoided by a clear path.

Approach
Almost invariably reached over A' Chralaig. Follow the ridge north over a subsidiary top to the saddle. The ridge ahead is narrow but easy at first, then there are a few optional easy scrambles before the pinnacles are reached.

The Route
Follow the crest over the sharp first pinnacle. A path now avoids all difficulties on the left, but the crest is better. Climb the next steep tower either direct on steep jugs (Grade 2) or by squeezing through a gap on the left, then up right to the arête. Crossing the top of the tower is airy, then descend on the right. The rest is easy.

SGURR NAN CONBHAIREAN

1109m   OS Landranger 34   (NH 129 138)

A graceful peak with pleasant grassy ridges and a prominent spur falling north-east into the wild upper reaches of Glen Doe.

120 North-East Spur   Grade 2   **
Alt 750m   East facing   (NH 135 138)   Map p212   Diagram p222

A good line linking outcrops up an airily-positioned spur. There is some exposure, but with positive holds.

Approach
The easiest approach is to climb Carn Ghluasaid and descend northwards from the Glas Bhealach south-east of the summit of Sgurr nan Conbhairean. Descend the upper corrie until it drops away steeply, then start at a jagged buttress on the left (west) just above the drop.

The Route
The central rib can be climbed at a loose Difficult, or an easier rib to the right followed. Boulders lead to a flattening, then go right under steep cliflets. Climb a long rib up the right-hand side of these on jugs, finishing with a patterned slab. Go up another easy rib, then go right to climb a series of ribs on the skyline. At a steeper section go up left from the lowest point by a juggy rib and a vegetated weakness. Follow the skyline easily, then move right to a slab poised above the drop on the right. Carry on up the nose on positive holds to an easing. Above climb a steeper buttress direct on good holds. Steep walking leads to the summit. In spring the top of this ridge can develop an impressive snow crest, giving the route an almost alpine feel.

KINTAIL

SGURR NAN CONBHAIREAN

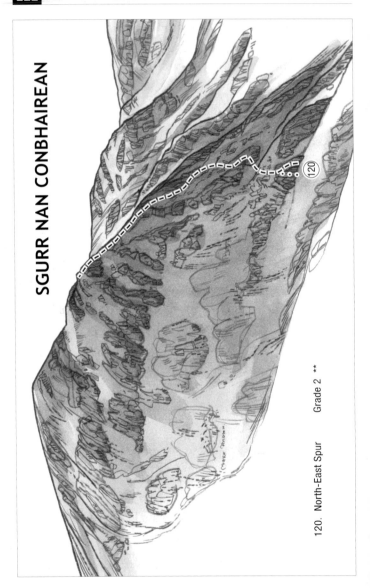

120. North-East Spur   Grade 2 **

AONACH AIR CHRITH

1021m   OS Landranger 33   (NH 051 083)

The popular Cluanie Ridge has several enjoyably narrow subsidiary ridges, the best being on Aonach Air Chrith.

121 North Ridge   Grade 1 or 2   *
Alt 450m   North facing   (NH 058 101)   Map p212

A route in two parts, a series of outcrops (Grade 2) then a narrow ridge (Grade 1). The first part can easily be bypassed by traversing in to the saddle beyond A' Chioch from the north-west.

Approach
From the layby at NH 044 114 follow the good path towards Druim Coire nan Eirecheanach. At around the 300m contour head south-west across the Allt Coire an Eirecheanach to the outcrops starting at around 450m on the north end of A' Chioch, the broad rounded top north of Aonach Air Chrith (unnamed on the 1:50,000 map). Start at the lowest slab, on its right.

The Route
Climb the furthest right-hand edge of the slab, then minor craglets lead up to a larger outcrop with an overhanging prow and a big groove on its left. Climb the left edge of the groove, steep at the top, then traverse right along a shelf below a vertical wall. Clamber onto the right-hand end of this to reach open ground. A short wall on the left is worth including before a grassy walk up to another larger outcrop. Go right of this and up its right-hand edge, finishing through a slot, then more grass leads to the top of A' Chioch.

   Cross the saddle ahead and go up right to join the north ridge proper, which is narrow and rocky. Keep on the crest for the most fun, passing over a minor top, from where two flaky towers and a narrow arête lead to the main summit.

SGURR NA SGINE

946m   OS Landranger 33   (NG 946 113)

A steep hill with a pleasant curving ridge, although rather overshadowed by The Saddle. The described scramble makes a good follow-on to the Forcan Ridge.

122 North-East Ridge   Grade 2
Alt 750m   North-East facing   (NG 948 115)   Map p212   Diagram p224

A short steep ridge on rough quartzy rock, quite exposed but easy.

Approach
The route can be approached directly up Coire Toiteil, but it is better to

SGURR NA SGINE

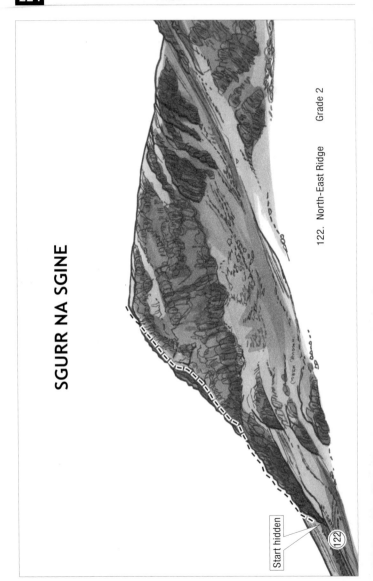

Start hidden

122

122. North-East Ridge   Grade 2

include it after the Forcan Ridge. Descend to the Bealach Coire Mhalagain, then go up steeply to the col between Sgurr na Sgine and Faochag. Turn right, then head left along an obvious shelf crossing the north face. Where this ends slant down to reach a very steep outcrop at the foot of the north-east ridge, the lowest rock on the face, with large boulders below it. Start just beyond this at quartzy rock, the right-hand of two ribs. This point can also be easily reached from the saddle between Sgurr na Sgine and Sgurr a' Bhac Chaolais.

The Route
Climb steeply onto the quartzy rib and follow it up, quite exposed at times. Where it ends go up steep vegetation and minor craglets until a sharp ridge develops. Follow this up on big flakes and boulders to arrive directly at the summit cairn.

THE SADDLE

1010m   OS Landranger 33   (NG 936 131)

A superb hill with three craggy ridges, the best of which is the famous Forcan Ridge. The circuit of the whole hill is a great long day, while a shorter but still excellent route takes in just the Forcan Ridge before moving across to the neighbouring Munro, Sgurr na Sgine, and climbing its north-east ridge as described above.

123 Forcan Ridge   Grade 2   ***
Alt 650m   East facing   (NG 947 131)   Map p212
One of the best scrambles in Scotland, a knife-edged ridge, quite exposed but not difficult. All the awkward bits can be avoided at Grade 1, but this misses out the best bits of the route.

Approach
A good stalkers' path leaves the A87 at NG 968 143. Follow this up to pass right of Meallan Odhar to the foot of the ridge.

The Route
A short well-used slab starts the scrambling (harder options exist to the right). An obvious route zigzags up through outcrops until the ridge bends right then left at around 800m. The ridge now narrows, with easier options on the right. A short tower at around 850m is passed by an exposed step up left, then just before the summit of Sgurr na Forcan itself another tower is climbed direct on steep flakes. Both these can be avoided on the right.

   The descent from Sgurr na Forcan is steep and intimidating but on good holds. This is the hardest part of the route, but there are easier options down gullies on both left and right. A slabby knife edge (avoidable on the left) leads to a minor top, then more broken scrambling leads to the main top of the Saddle, with the slightly lower trig point just beyond.

KINTAIL

Iain Thow on the Forcan Ridge (Grade 2), The Saddle
Photo: Iain Thow collection

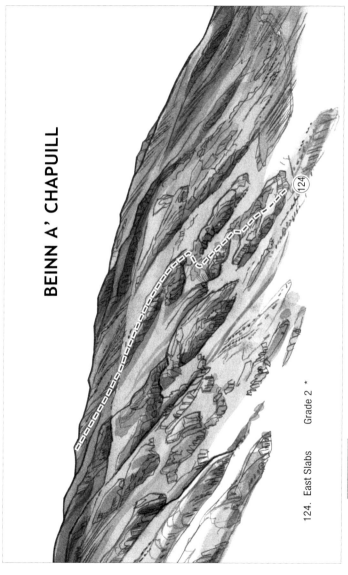

BEINN A' CHAPUILL

124. East Slabs   Grade 2 *

BEINN A' CHAPUILL

759m   OS Landranger 33   (NG 835 148)

This knobbly plateau north-west of Beinn Sgritheall has a lot of rock on its steep sides, as well as being an excellent viewpoint. There is scope for far more scrambling than just the route described, while the north-east ridge is a delightful walk up from Gleann Beag.

124 East Slabs   Grade 2   *
Alt 450m   East facing   (NG 837 146)   Map p212   Diagram p227

A steep hillside scattered with gneiss slabs, giving lots of route choice. Harder variations can easily be found.

Approach
Start from the forest track leaving the road at NG 780 136 (parking 50 metres up the track). Follow the track through the wood, then keep ahead up the Allt Gorm and cross over to Loch Bealach na h-Oidhche. From the saddle north-east of this traverse northwards, descending slightly. Pass under the first slabs, which are steep and often wet, to reach cleaner lower slabs slanting up left.

The Route
Climb the right-hand side of the lowest rib (the flaky crack just left of the foot is Difficult). Carry on up slabs until they run out into the hillside. Traverse right below boulders and up more slabs. Follow these onto the next open buttress, with a wide choice of route. Link together slabs and boulder problems until the rock starts to peter out. Bear up left to reach more clean slabs which provide a nice finish, arriving at the plateau just south-east of the summit lochan. A slightly lower top marked Beinn a' Chapuill (742m) on OS maps lies a further 750 metres north-west.

THE OUTER HEBRIDES

All the Outer Hebrides are rocky, as the Lewisian gneiss produces some of the roughest hills in the country, with rock outcropping all over the place. Much of it is easy-angled, but many of the steeper faces give superb scrambling. The wildly indented coastline of the islands means that the sea is everywhere, giving stunning views and an 'edge of the world' atmosphere.

The described routes are in three well-separated areas, the Uig Hills in West Lewis, the central knot of mountains in Harris and a couple of minor routes on the more isolated peaks on South Uist. The Uig Hills are best accessed via the Ullapool to Stornaway ferry, the Harris routes from Skye via the Uig to Tarbert ferry and the South Uist hills via either the Uig to Lochmaddy or Oban to Lochboisdale services. A ferry runs from Leverburgh to Berneray linking Harris and the Uists and Calmac offer various 'Island Hopscotch' tickets which can be much cheaper than the standard fare. Bus services link Stornoway with Tarbert and Leverburgh and Berneray with Lochmaddy and Lochboisdale, plus a minibus service from Stornoway to Uig (all Mon–Sat, information from Stornoway Bus Station 01851 704327).

All three islands have different characters. Much of Lewis is blanketed in deep peat, but in the south-west corner the Uig Hills are as rocky as any scrambler could wish. They consist of two north–south ridges with rounded summits and steep sides, giving acres of slabby scrambling on excellent gneiss. There are many more possibilities than those described. Harris is not dissimilar, but the hills are higher and more crowded together, giving more of a big mountain feel. The Gillaval Dubh routes in particular are amongst the best in this guide. The South Uist hills are more vegetated and the scrambling minor. The impressive looking Hellisdale (Sheileasdail) Buttresses on Beinn Mhor are frighteningly loose, although all have been climbed.

Although only a few miles apart the east and west coasts often have totally different weather, so good route choice can pay dividends here. Finally it must be said that any visit to Lewis, Harris or Uist would be incomplete without a visit to at least one of the west coast's magnificent beaches, as beautiful as any in the world (just a pity about the water temperature!).

West Lewis
Map p230

Most of Lewis is fairly low, but south of the major indentation of Loch Roag the coast is dominated by the rocky Uig Hills, two lines of ice-scraped gneiss summits offering endless scope for scrambling and a few harder possibilities. Nearby are the Uig sea cliffs, with vast numbers of rock climbs. In particular, many users of this guide might be interested in Sunset Ridge (Difficult), an excellent short route up an obvious strip of pink pegmatite. The top of the sea cliffs also makes a very enjoyable evening stroll.

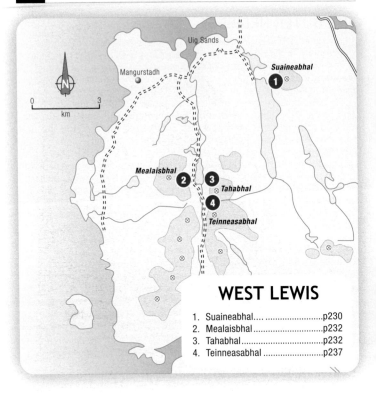

WEST LEWIS

SUAINEABHAL

429m   OS Landranger 13   (NB 077 309)

An isolated summit to the north-east of the main Uig group with a craggy west face and outstanding views.

125 West Slabs   Grade 3   **

Alt 50m West facing (NB 071 305)   Map p230   Diagram p231

Slabs to start, then steeper outcrops, all on excellent gneiss.

Approach

From the foot of Loch Suaineabhal (NB 064 310) cross the weir and follow the loch shore round until below Suaineabhal. The first cliffs are steep, but 100 metres further on a slabby spur comes down close to the loch, with a cairn on a boulder at its foot.

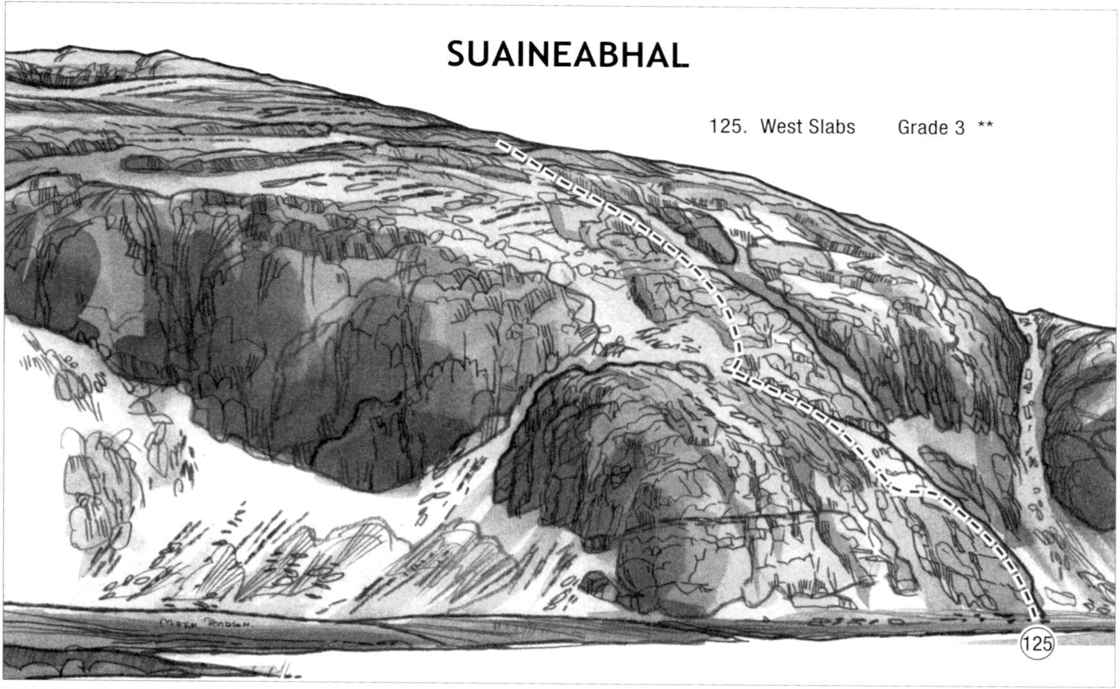

SUAINEABHAL

125. West Slabs   Grade 3 **

The Route
Go up left of a prominent vertical crack, then up excellent slabs above. Pull over a small overhang on the right, then go up more slabs, with the rib becoming better defined. Where it ends walk left across a heathery hollow to another slabby rib. This is delicate at first, then easier up the line of a thin crack. Walk up to a steeper outcrop. The shattered crack in this is harder than it looks and better avoided on the left. Another steep tier is climbed by a groove with a hard start. Go up right to the next craglet and climb it by a knobbly groove. Broken steps above are still quite steep, then the ground eases to slabs. Above these follow a left-trending set of ribs to the top of the face. Minor problems can be found on the way to the summit.

MEALAISBHAL

574m   OS Landranger 13   (NB 021 270)

The highest hill in Lewis, its northern spur has a steep vegetated cliff on its north side, named Creagan Tealasdale on the 1:25,000 map. The left-hand edge of the face is a broad slabby buttress of excellent gneiss.

126 East Buttress   Grade 2   **
Alt 100m   North-East facing   (NB 032 280)   Map p230   Diagram p233
Open slabs, not exposed, with difficulties all avoidable. One steeper step borders on Grade 3.

Approach
Follow the private vehicle track from NB 032 313 as far as Loch Mor na Clibhe (locked gate at the crossing of the Abhainn Stocaill). Go right and follow the south side of the loch, passing under the first slabs to more slabs forming the left edge of the main north face.

The Route
The slabs are easy at first, steepening briefly before a more serious bulge left of a square tower. Climb a crack just left of centre, then go right to left up a short steep wall on good holds. Climb another short wall on the right, then a nose at a pointed flake. Continue up the crest to a grassy shoulder, then small outcrops just left of the crest lead up to the top of the cliff. The last step has a flake crack in its nose, giving an optional hard finish (Difficult).

TAHABHAL

515m   OS Landranger 13   (NB 042 263)

An exceptionally rocky hill, with the whole of the north and west faces giving scrambling, and occasionally harder routes. The clean rib at the right-hand end of the north face and the slabs and overlaps on the south-west corner are particularly good.

MEALAISBHAL
North-East Face

126. East Buttress   Grade 2 **

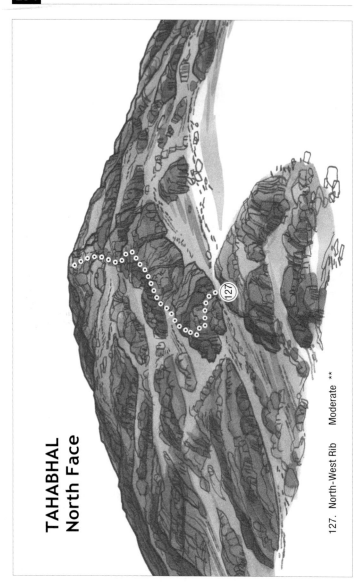

TAHABHAL
North Face

127. North-West Rib   Moderate **

127 North-West Rib   Moderate   **

Alt 300m   North facing   (NB 043 268)   Map p230   Diagram p234

A steep rib with some quite hard sections, occasionally exposed. Even better with a direct finish, but this is Very Difficult.

Approach

As for Route 126 to Loch Mor na Clibhe, then cross the river at the foot of Loch Raonasgail and slant up south-east to the western edge of the saddle north of Tahabhal. The route is the almost continuous rib on the right-hand edge of the North Face. A few broken outcrops below it can be bypassed or included to reach an overhanging block at the foot of the rib proper.

The Route

Gain the top of the initial face easily from the right, then go up a steep chimney on the left and follow steps up leftwards. Go up the right-hand side of the nose above to easy ground. Follow the crest up short steps, then move right onto an exposed arête above steep slabs. Follow this up right to a grass ledge, then go up a quartzy crack to a terrace.

Move left and go up a stepped arête, then climb the left arête of a wet V-groove (quite hard). A slabby arête leads to boulders, then climb a rib on the right. Easy slabs now lead to a more substantial buttress.

Thrutch up the obvious wide crack, then climb flakes and a slab above to a ledge below the final face. A slab and crack directly above are Very Difficult, so for a more consistent finish walk 10m up left, then go up the left edge and over a small overhang. Step up right to a delicate ramp, make a couple of moves up left on this, then make an airy move up right to the top.

128 South-West Shoulder   Moderate   **

Alt 200m   South-West facing   (NB 038 262)   Map p230   Diagram p236

A varied and sustained series of problems on clean granite, very reminiscent of Arran. Strenuous in places but not exposed.

Approach

Follow the vehicle track as for Route 126 until about 0.5km beyond the south end of Loch Raonasgail. Go steeply uphill to the lowest spur of slabs descending from the cliffs up on the left. Go diagonally up left 20 metres to the next spur and start there.

The Route

Climb the left edge of the slabs until they finish, then transfer to the next set and follow these up right to a steep wall. Either make a precarious step left around this and go up or avoid it on the right. Gain the next slab from the left, then the next by a wide crack on the left and climb it direct. Climb a chimney in a nose, then the next nose by flakes. Another slab then leads to an apparent impasse.

Traverse right across big boulders into a slabby niche below vertical walls, then climb a strenuous chimney in the back (don't miss the very useful

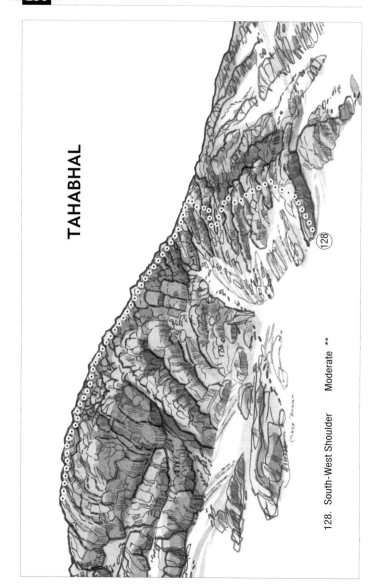

TAHABHAL

128. South-West Shoulder   Moderate **

foothold out on the right arête!). Take the left fork of the chimney, then slant right up slabs to the right-hand edge of the cliff. Just before this go left up flakes to the crest.

Carry on up the crest, then big flakes lead up left to a gash running horizontally left. Go through this and up slabs. Follow more flakes up left and regain the crest. Go horizontally left below a huge block and up jugs behind it. The ridge now starts to break up into enormous blocks, giving problems of every conceivable grade. Generally work up left, with huge flakes, ramps and the odd strenuous crack providing plenty of entertainment. The easiest versions are generally on the right. The problems finally peter out only a few metres below the summit.

TEINNEASABHAL

497m   OS Landranger 13   (NB 041 253)

Sgorran Dubh Teinneasabhal dominates the upper reaches of Gleann Raonasgail. The best climbing is on its Far South Buttress, but the sprawling North Buttress gives a good scramble.

129 North Buttress   Grade 3   *
Alt 200m   West facing   (NB 037 255)   Map p230   Diagram p238

An intricate but logical line up a big face, mostly slabby but with some steeper sections. Many harder variations possible.

Approach
As for Route 126 but stay on the track until 1km beyond the head of Loch Raonasgail. The face up left is split by a prominent central Y-gully. North Buttress is the broad face on its left, with preliminary slabs below. Go up to the right-hand base of these.

The Route
Start up the right-hand side of a short step at the foot of the slabs, then move left onto them and slant up right to the edge. Go up a slabby rib on the right-hand edge, then move left onto more slabs. Go rightwards up these to grass. Easy slabby ribs lead to more grass below the steep main face.

Walk 20 metres right to a clean rib on the skyline. Go up this, then steeper steps trending up right to grass. Move right again and climb another slabby rib, with a useful crack on the right at the steepest part. At steeper rock work up right across grooves to the right-hand edge, then go back up left. Easier rock now leads up the centre of a broad spur to another steepening. Climb this by a groove full of spikes. Go up the right-hand arête of the next groove then follow the crest of the spur. Swing left onto a ramp below a steep wall, then go up right onto its top. Move left again and climb a series of short steps to the top. The summit is only a few metres away.

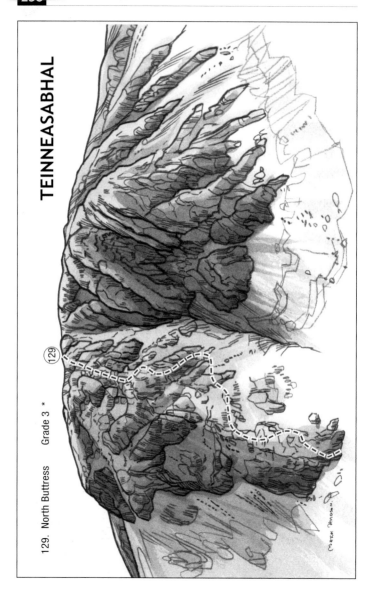

TEINNEASABHAL

129. North Buttress   Grade 3 *

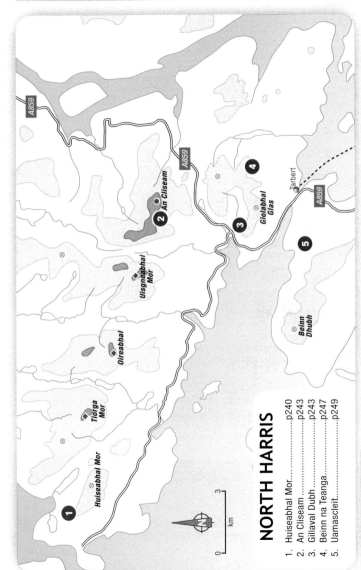

NORTH HARRIS

Harris

Map p239

Although physically part of the same island as Lewis, Harris has a startlingly different character. It is much hillier and more rugged, with An Cliseam rising to nearly 800m. North of the isthmus at Tarbert, North Harris consists of several north–south ridges with steep sides, many of which have areas of cliff, the most impressive being the huge overhanging pillar of Sron Uladal. South Harris, on the other hand, has more isolated smaller hills with fewer scrambling possibilities, as well as having the lion's share of the beaches. Worth a visit in passing is the north-east shoulder of Roineabhal, which has steep slabs on its right-hand side.

HUISEABHAL MOR

489m   OS Landranger 13   (NB 022 116)

This ridge at the west end of the North Harris hills falls steeply into Glen Cravadale to the north. The face is very vegetated, but there is good scrambling at the west end, the best being the following route.

 130 Cravadale Rib   Grade 3   *
Alt 200m   North facing   (NB 009 129)   Map p239   Diagram p241

A short but excellent scramble with great views, quite sustained.

Approach

From the road end at Huisinis (parking at NA 993 121) take the path around northwards over the top of the first cliffs, then across a col to Loch na Cleabhaig. From the cottage go up left of the stream towards a prominent steep buttress on the skyline. Link easy-angled slabs to reach a shelf at the bottom of this.

The Route

Left of the small overhangs at the bottom are steep slabs, then left again is a grass shelf a few feet up. Pull up onto this and climb cracks above. At the top of the buttress these steepen, forcing a delicate traverse left to the edge and up to a moss and heather shelf. This point can also be reached by climbing the right-hand edge of the buttress (Difficult).

   Climb the right-hand edge of the steep buttress above on good holds, finishing up a thin crack. Easier slabs then lead to another shelf. Move left and climb the buttress above a small leaning wall to the top. A few more outcrops can be found up and left.

The parallel ridge to the left has some easy scrambling (Grade 1). The rib left again is enjoyably slabby with plenty of route choice, starting up a subsidiary spur below and left (Grade 2).

HUISEABHAL MOR

130. Cravadale Rib   Grade 3 *

130

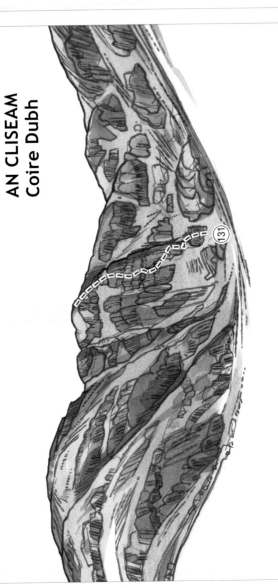

AN CLISEAM
Coire Dubh

131. Coire Dubh Slabs   Grade 3 **

AN CLISEAM (CLISHAM)

799m   OS Landranger 14   (NB 154 073)

The highest peak in the Outer Hebrides, An Cliseam consists of a north-east facing horseshoe, with the summit on the southern arm. There is some scrambling on the ridge to Mulla-Fo-Dheas, mostly just boulders, but with some Grade 1 slabs just right of the skyline. The best scrambling, however, is on the headwall of Coire Dubh just south of this.

131 Coire Dubh Slabs   Grade 3   **

Alt 400m   South facing   (NB 146 074)   Map p239   Diagram p242

Prominent from a distance, these clean gneiss slabs lead up to a minor top on the ridge. The rib left of the slabs is Grade 2, with much variation possible. Avoid the overhangs at half height by pink steps on the left.

Approach

Either follow the path up from Bun Abhainn Eadarra before breaking up right into Coire Dubh, or traverse in over Tarsabhal from where the road levels off at NB 160 052. The slabs are obvious, central on the back wall of the corrie. Below the right-hand edge is a broken rib. Start here, at a gritty slab below a short steep broken wall.

The Route

Climb the gritty slab and the left-hand edge of the steeper wall, then follow the rib and slabs above until they peter out. Go left and climb another rib to reach a rake slanting up left below the main sweep of cleaner steeper slabs. Follow the rake up left to a large grass patch, go up this and keep bearing left up broken steps below the cleaner slabs to reach grassy ledges leading off left.

  Climb the slabs above by cracks left of a blank slab. On the right is a more crystalline slab. Climb this bearing left and crossing a small overlap to reach steeper slabs with a left-curving overlap. Climb steep cracks left of this, then go more easily up left to a reddish crystalline band. Climb this rightwards (serious), then go left up slabs to reach greyer smoother rock. Go direct up this to reach more broken ground. Above this a square-cut rib on the right is excellent, then easy ground with the odd problem leads to the skyline. A steep subsidiary rib on the left makes an interesting finish.

GILLAVAL DUBH

417m   OS Landranger 14   (NB 140 027)

The north face of this hill consists of a row of six buttresses up to 250m high overlooking the Tarbert to Stornoway road, reached by a steep 15–20 minute walk. Described from the left: A, C and D Buttresses are all excellent scrambles on superb gneiss, E and F Buttresses are short and easy (F with a

Peter Duggan on the upper section of Coire Dubh Slabs (Grade 3), An Cliseam
Photo: Noel Williams

hard start, Grade 3), while B is cut by a series of steep greasy walls, forcing scramblers onto insecure vegetated ground.

132 A Buttress   Grade 2 or 3   *
Alt 150m   North facing   (NB 142 029)   Map p239   Diagram p246

A broad buttress with much choice of route, grassy in places, but with some excellent slabby ribs.

Approach

From the bridge over the Skeaudale River (NB 138 034) go up south-east to the left-hand of the six buttresses (it forms the skyline from the bridge). There are a few isolated slabs low down, but start above these, on the left-hand side of the main buttress, just left of the lowest point, below a steep red wall about 6m up.

The Route

Go up left of the steep red wall. Easy rocks follow with the stepped blocky rib in the centre providing a good route. At the overhang go up left and climb the left-hand side of the tier. Continue up to a large projecting boulder, then go up right and climb stepped slabs. These are steep at the top (Grade 3), but easily dodged. Now choose between steep boulder problems on the left or easier ground to the right. Follow easy steps to a large shelf which slopes down into the gully on the right. Twin cracks on the right lead up a rib, then carry on up until the buttress peters out into open hillside. Go up right to the skyline and follow this up to finish up a superb juggy rib.

133 C Buttress   Grade 3   ***
Alt 150m   North facing   (NB 140 030)   Map p239   Diagram p246

Sustained scrambling on perfect gneiss, intimidating but easier than it looks.

Approach

From the bridge over the Skeaudale River at NB 138 034 go up south-east to the third buttress from the left. Start on the right, by the stream (often dry). There is a prominent little slab just right of the stream for an appetiser.

The Route

Go up slabs left of the stream to grass, then more slabs with a steeper move in the middle. Walking and easy rock now lead to a steeper buttress. Start centrally and go up to a stepped wall. Follow a grass ledge out right, then slant right up awkward slabby steps to easy ground, quite exposed. More direct harder variations are feasible. Go up to the next slabs and up the superb rib in the centre. Go up left to steeper rocks on the skyline and climb the left-hand of two grooves, then move left to a lovely friction slab. The steep tier ahead is easiest by its left edge, but the juggy middle is easier than it looks. The buttress now narrows and small steps lead to an imposing central crack (again, easier than it seems). The vertical wall above is dodged on the left, then broken slabs lead to the top.

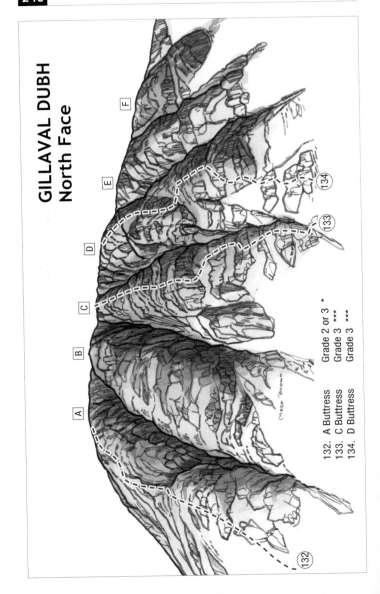

GILLAVAL DUBH
North Face

A B C D E F

132. A Buttress   Grade 2 or 3 *
133. C Buttress   Grade 3 ***
134. D Buttress   Grade 3 ***

134 D Buttress   Grade 3   ★★★
Alt 150m   North facing   (NB 139 030)   Map p239   Diagram p246
Quite hard to start, but easier than it looks. Sustained and on excellent rock.

Approach
From the bridge over the Skeaudale River at NB 138 034 go up south-east to the fourth buttress from the left. Start at the largest area of slabs at the bottom left of the buttress.

The Route
Climb the slabs, steep but with good friction, to a heather terrace. Go up a slabby rib on the right, then up grass to a steeper buttress. Start up steps on the left and move into the centre as the angle eases. Climb steeper more awkward slabs (crux, with the remains of an old peg), then go up left of a vertical wall to grass ledges. This section can be bypassed by taking a good ledge rightwards and climbing the right-hand edge of the buttress.

   Go right up grass to the skyline, then climb steeper rocks centrally, up a nose and a mossy groove to easier ground. Follow easy slabs until a grassy gully comes in from the left and splits the buttress. Traverse left to climb a rib (the avoidable bulge at the bottom is Difficult). Carry on up the slabby rib, passing right of two overhangs, until this gives out to grass. Boulders on the left lead to a nose, passed on the right. The next rib is gained steeply from the right, then more slabs lead to the top, with an optional overlap on the left halfway up.

BEINN NA TEANGA

440m   OS Landranger 14   (NB 160 026)

A minor top at the head of Glen Skeaudale, with rough spurs running south and south-east enclosing Gleann Lingeadail.

 135 Lingeadail Slabs   Grade 1
Alt 300m   South-West facing   (NB 166 024)   Map p239
Gently-angled slabs add interest to a wild hillwalk. Much harder when wet.

Approach
From the south end of the Laxadale track (NB 177 004) traverse up north-west past Loch Torascleit. The slabs line the north-east side of the top end of Gleann Lingeadail. Start at the right-hand (lowest) end.

The Route
Slant left up the easy lower slabs to a heather shelf, aiming for a prominent stepped corner on the upper tier. Above the shelf climb more slabs bearing up left to a smaller shelf below the corner. Climb smooth slabs left of the corner and go up steps to its top. Clean ribs on the right make a good continuation.

UAMASCLEIT

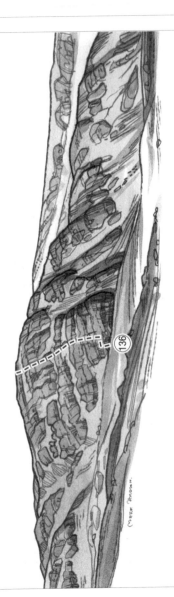

136. North-East Face   Grade 3 *

UAMASCLEIT

281m OS Landranger 14 (NB 127 996)

A minor top overlooking West Loch Tarbert, accessible, but with quite a remote feel. One of the few scrambles in South Harris.

 136 North-East Face Grade 3 *

Alt 100m North facing (NB 130 000) Map p239 Diagram p248

Called the eastern top of Ben Luskentyre in the climbing guide. Avoid the steep lower slabs by an exposed traverse to reach easier ribs of excellent rock.

Approach

All approaches are rough and wet, but best is to follow the south shore of West Loch Tarbert from behind the school (NB 149 002). Where the steep shoreline falls back cut south-west across bogs to the cliff. Start at the left-hand end of the clean rock, left of the overhangs.

The Route

Go up an easy subsidiary slab left of the crag, then go right up heather to take a narrow exposed ledge horizontally right just above the main cliff. Climb a superb slabby rib and where this ends go up right to climb juggy slabs right of a steeper rib to a large shelf. An easy rib with a tiny overhang at the bottom leads to another shelf, then climb the next rib in a series of steps. Ahead is a steep slab of extreme roughness, then an easier slabby rib leads to the top.

South Uist

Map p250

The long island of South Uist has a low west side fringed by splendid white beaches. The east side is a complete contrast, much wilder and rougher, with quite a remote feel. The rugged peaks of Beinn Mhor and Hecla dominate the island and make a splendid traverse with a little scrambling. The big cliffs above Gleann Sheileasdail impress from a distance but turn out to be very loose and vegetated. Many of the smaller hills are also very rocky, but it is hard to string the outcrops together into good scrambles.

BEINN CORRADAIL

527m OS Landranger 22 (NF 819 328)

Although usually viewed as just an incident in the traverse of Beinn Mhor and Hecla, Beinn Corradail is quite an individual peak. The north face is rocky but vegetated, while the face above Bealach Sheileasdail (shown as Sheiliosdail on OS maps) is quite craggy too.

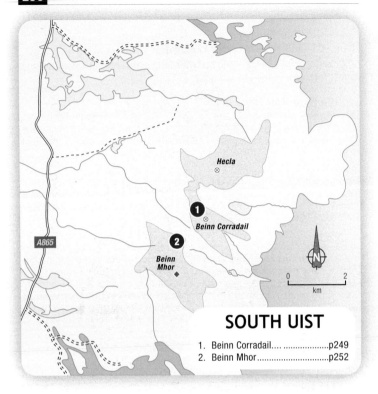

SOUTH UIST

137 North-West Ridge   Grade 2

Alt 500m   North-West facing   (NF 819 330)   Map p250   Diagram p251

Short but worth including if passing. A steep start leads to exposed but easy steps.

Approach

Most will traverse Hecla first, descending to the saddle at the head of Gleann Uisinis, but a direct approach uses the peat road starting at NF 767 346 and goes up Gleann Dorchaidh. In either case go up the grassy North-West Ridge to the twin buttresses just below the summit. Start at the right edge of the right-hand buttress, at a block, with a rocky gully to the right.

The Route

Climb a couple of steep steps, then move left onto the crest. Go up this, quite exposed at first, then the angle gradually eases to the summit.

BEINN CORRADAIL

137. North-West Ridge   Grade 2

BEINN MHOR

620m   OS Landranger 22   (NF 808 311)

The highest hill on South Uist, Beinn Mhor has an enjoyably narrow summit ridge, with huge but loose buttresses falling northwards into Gleann Sheileasdail.

 138 North-East Ridge   Grade 1
Alt 300m   North-East facing   (NF 813 323)   Map p250

A few minor outcrops make a pleasant way of gaining height.

Approach
Bealach Sheileasdail (Hellisdale) will usually be reached by traversing Hecla and Beinn Corradail, but could be reached directly up Gleann Dorchaidh from the peat road starting at NF 767 346. At the west end of the bealach is a notch, with a steep wall on the left (looking up).

The Route
Climb a stepped rib on the right end of the wall to walking-angle slabs. At another steep wall climb the left arête. Minor outcrops then lead to an easy slabby spur. Follow this, then more outcrops higher up.

Latin Names of Species
- mentioned in the wildlife chapter:

Flowering plants

alder	*Alnus glutinosa*
Alpine bistort	*Persicaria vivipara*
Alpine cinquefoil	*Potentilla crantzii*
Alpine lady's mantle	*Alchemilla alpina*
Alpine meadow-rue	*Thalictrum alpinum*
Alpine saw-wort	*Saussurea alpina*
Arctic bearberry	*Arctostaphylos alpinus*
ash	*Fraxinus excelsior*
awlwort	*Subularia aquatica*
bearberry	*Arctostaphylos uva-ursi*
bell-heather	*Erica cinerea*
bent grasses	*Agrostis* species
birch (downy)	*Betula pubescens*
black bog-rush	*Schoenus nigricans*
bladderworts	*Utricularia* species
blaeberry	*Vaccinium myrtillus*
bluebell	*Hyacinthoides non-scripta*
blue water-speedwell	*Veronica anagallis-aquatica*
bog asphodel	*Narthecium ossifragum*
bog bean	*Menyanthes trifoliata*
bog myrtle	*Myrica gale*
bottle sedge	*Carex rostrata*
broad-leaved cottongrass	*Eriophorum latifolium*
butterworts	*Pinguicula vulgaris and P. lusitanica*
common birds-foot-trefoil	*Lotus corniculatus*
common cottongrass	*Eriophorum angustifolium*
common spotted orchid	*Dactylorhiza maculata*
cowberry	*Vaccinium vitis-idaea*
cross-leaved heath	*Erica tetralix*
crowberry	*Empetrum nigrum*
dark red helleborine	*Epipactis atrorubens*
deer-grass	*Trichophorum cespitosum*
devil's-bit scabious	*Succisa pratensis*
dogs' mercury	*Mercurialis perennis*
downy willow	*Salix lapponum*
dwarf cornel	*Cornus suecica*
dwarf cudweed	*Gnaphalium supinum*
dwarf juniper	*Juniperus communis* ssp. *nana*
dwarf willow	*Salix herbacea*
eared willow	*Salix aurita*

eyebrights	*Euphrasia* species
fairy flax	*Linum catharticum*
fescue grasses	*Festuca* species
frog orchid	*Coeloglossum viride*
globeflower	*Trollius europaeaus*
goldenrod	*Solidago virgaurea*
grass of Parnassus	*Parnassia palustris*
greater woodrush	*Luzula sylvatica*
hazel	*Corylus avellana*
heath bedstraw	*Galium saxatile*
heather	*Calluna vulgaris*
heath milkwort	*Polygala serpyllifolia*
lesser twayblade orchid	*Listera cordata*
lousewort	*Pedicularis sylvatica*
mare's-tail	*Hippuris vulgaris*
mat-grass	*Nardus stricta*
meadowsweet	*Filipendula ulmaria*
melancholy thistle	*Cirsium helenioides*
moss campion	*Silene acaulis*
mossy cyphel	*Minuartia sedoides*
mountain avens	*Dryas octopetala*
mountain azalea	*Loiseleuria procumbens*
mountain everlasting	*Antennaria dioica*
net-leaved willow	*Salix reticulata*
northern bedstraw	*Galium boreale*
oak (sessile)	*Quercus petraea*
purple moor-grass	*Molinia caerulea*
roseroot	*Rhodiola rosea*
rowan	*Sorbus aucuparia*
sanicle	*Sanicula europaea*
Scots lovage	*Ligusticum scoticum*
Scots pine	*Pinus sylvestris*
Scottish asphodel	*Tofieldia pusilla*
Scottish primrose	*Primula scotica*
scurvy grass	*Cochlearia officianalis*
sea campion	*Silene uniflora*
sea plantain	*Plantago maritima*
shoreweed	*Littorella uniflora*
Sibbaldia	*Sibbaldia procumbens*
spiked wood-rush	*Luzula spicata*
spring squill	*Scilla verna*
starry saxifrage	*Saxifraga stellaris*
stiff sedge	*Carex bigelowii*
sundews	*Drosera* species
three-leaved rush	*Juncus trifidus*

thrift	*Armeria maritima*
tormentil	*Potentilla erecta*
viviparous fescue	*Festuca vivipara*
water avens	*Geum rivale*
water lobelia	*Lobelia dortmanna*
white water-lily	*Nymphaea alba*
whortle-leaved willow	*Salix myrsinites*
wild angelica	*Angelica sylvestris*
wild garlic	*Allium ursinum*
wild thyme	*Thymus polytrichus*
wood cranesbill	*Geranium sylvaticum*
woolly willow	*Salix lanata*
yellow iris	*Iris pseudacorus*
yellow saxifrage	*Saxifraga aizoides*

Non-flowering plants

alpine clubmoss	*Diphasiastrum alpinum*
bog mosses	*Sphagnum* species
brown seaweeds (a type of Algae)	(family *Phaeophyceae*)
fir clubmoss	*Huperzia selago*
holly fern	*Polystichum lonchitis*
Icelandic reindeer-moss (lichen)	*Cetraria islandica*
moonwort (fern)	*Botrychium lunaria*
fountain apple-moss	*Philonotis fontana*
hooked scorpion-moss	*Scorpidium scorpioides*
parsley fern	*Cryptogramma crispa*
sea spleenwort (fern)	*Asplenium marinum*
stag's-horn clubmoss	*Lycopodium clavatum*
stoneworts (a type of Algae)	(family *Characeae*)
water horsetail	*Equisetum fluviatile*
woolly fringe-moss	*Racomitrium lanuginosum*

Birds

black-throated diver	*Gavia arctica*
buzzard	*Buteo buteo*
carrion crow	*Corvus corone corone*
common sandpiper	*Actitis hypoleucos*
cuckoo	*Cuculus canorus*
curlew	*Numenius arquata*
dipper	*Cinclus cinclus*
dotterel	*Charadrius morinellus*
fulmar	*Fulmarus glacialis*
goldcrest	*Regulus regulus*
golden eagle	*Aquila chrysaetos*
golden plover	*Pluvialis apricaria*

greenshank	*Tringa nebularia*
grouse (red)	*Lagopus lagopus scoticus*
guillemot	*Uria aalge*
hen harrier	*Circus cyaneus*
hooded crow	*Corvus corone cornix*
kittiwake	*Rissa tridactyla*
lapwing	*Vanellus vanellus*
meadow pipit	*Anthus pratensis*
merlin	*Falco columbarius*
oystercatcher	*Haematopus ostralegus*
peregrine falcon	*Falco peregrinus*
ptarmigan	*Lagopus mutus*
raven	*Corvus corax*
razorbill	*Alca torda*
redshank	*Tringa totanus*
redstart	*Phoenicurus phoenicurus*
red-throated diver	*Gavia stellata*
ring ouzel	*Turdus torquatus*
short-eared owl	*Asio flammeus*
snow bunting	*Plectrophenax nivalis*
stonechat	*Saxicola torquata*
wheatear	*Oenanthe oenanthe*
whinchat	*Saxicola rubetra*
wood warbler	*Phylloscopus sibilatrix*

Mammals

American mink	*Mustela vison*
bottle-nosed dolphin	*Tursiops truncatus*
common (harbour) seal	*Phoca vitulina*
feral goat	*Capra hircus*
field vole	*Microtus agrestis*
fox	*Vulpes vulpes*
grey (Atlantic) seal	*Halichoerus grypus*
harbour porpoise	*Phocoena phocoena*
minke whale	*Balaenoptera acutorostra*
mole	*Talpa europaea*
mountain hare	*Lepus timidus*
otter	*Lutra lutra*
pine marten	*Martes martes*
rabbit	*Oryctolagus cuniculus*
red deer	*Cervus elaphus*
roe deer	*Capreolus capreolus*
water vole	*Arvicola terrestris*
wildcat	*Felis silvestris*

Reptiles & amphibians

adder	*Vipera berus*
common frog	*Rana temporaria*
common lizard	*Lacerta vivipara*
slow worm	*Anguis fragilis*

Fish

Arctic charr	*Salvelinus alpinus*
Atlantic salmon	*Salmo salar*
brown trout	*Salmo trutta*
sea trout	*Salmo trutta*

Invertebrates

azure hawker (dragonfly)	*Aeshna caerulea*
damselflies	order *Odonata*
dark green fritillary butterfly	*Argynnis aglaja*
dragonflies	order *Odonata*
emperor moth	*Saturnia pavonia*
freshwater pearl mussel	*Margaritifera margaritifera*
large heath butterfly	*Coenonympha tullia*
midge	*Culicoides* species
northern eggar moth	*Lasiocampa quercus callunae*

FURTHER READING

History/General
The Age of the Clans
R Dodgshon. Birlinn (2002)

Beinn Eighe – the Mountain above the Wood
JL Johnston & R Balharry. Birlinn (2001)

Celtic Scotland
I Armit. Batsford (1997)

The Drove Roads of Scotland
ARB Haldane. Birlinn (1997)

Exploring the Far North West of Scotland
R Gilbert. Cordee (1994)

Exploring the North and West Highlands
R Noble. Scottish Cultural Press (2003)

Glenelg, Kintail & Lochalsh
R Miket. Maclean Press (1998)

Harris in History and Legend
B Lawson. John Donald (2002)

The Highland Clearances
J Prebble. Penguin (2000)

Hills of the North Rejoice!
R MacGregor. Curlew Cottage Books (2000)

Isolation Shepherd
IR Thomson. Bidean Books (1983)

Lonely Hills and Wilderness Trails
R Gilbert. David & Charles (2000)

The Making of the Crofting Community
J Hunter. Edinburgh (1976)

The North West Highlands
T Atkinson. Luath Press (1999)

The Picts and the Scots
L & J Laing. Alan Sutton (1993)

Ralph's Far North
R MacGregor. Curlew Cottage Books (2004)

The Road to Mingulay
D Cooper. Warner Books (1985)

Scotland's First Settlers
CR Wickham-Jones. Batsford (1994)

Touring Scotland – Wester Ross
R Findlay. Foulis (1971)

Geology

Excursion Guide to the Geology of East Sutherland and Caithness
Edited by NH Trewin & A Hurst. Geological Society of Aberdeen (1993)

An Excursion Guide to the Moine Geology of the Scottish Highlands
Edited by I Allison, F May and RA Strachan. Scottish Academic Press (1988)

Exploring the Landscape of Assynt (Guide and Map)
K Goodenough, E Pickett, M Krabbendam & T Bradwell. British Geological
Survey (2004)

The Geological Structure of the Northwest Highlands of Scotland
BN Peach, J Horne, W Gunn, CT Clough, LW Hinxman & JJH Teall.
Memoir of the Geological Survey of Great Britain (1907)

Geology and Landscapes of Scotland
Con Gillen. Terra Publishing (2003)

The Geology of Scotland (4th Edition)
Edited by Nigel H. Trewin. The Geological Society, London (2002)

The Highland Geology Trail
JL Roberts. Luath Press (1998)

The Northern Highlands of Scotland (4th Edition)
GS Johnstone & W Mykura. British Geological Survey, HMSO (1989)

Northwest Highlands – A landscape fashioned by geology
J Mendum, J Merritt & A McKirdy. Scottish Natural Heritage (2001)

Scotland: The Creation of its Natural Landscape
A McKirdy & R Crofts. Scottish Natural Heritage (1999)

<http://earth.leeds.ac.uk/assyntgeology>

Speleology

Caves of Assynt
Edited by TJ Lawson. The Grampian Speleological Group (1988)

Wildlife

Flora of Assynt
PA Evans, IM Evans & GP Rothero. Privately published (2002)

Flora of the Outer Hebrides
RJ Pankhurst & JM Mullin. HMSO, London (1994)

The Hebrides
JM Boyd & IL Boyd. Collins New Naturalist, London (1990)

The Highlands and Islands
FF Darling & JM Boyd. Collins New Naturalist, London (1964)

Mosses & Liverworts – Naturally Scottish series (see also other titles in series)
GP Rothero. Scottish Natural Heritage, Perth (2005)

Mountain Flowers
J Raven & M Walters. Collins New Naturalist, London (1971)

The Outer Hebrides – Moor and Machair
S Angus. White Horse Press, Harris and Cambridge (2001)

Torridon, the Nature of the Place
C Lowe. Wester Ross Net, Shieldaig (2000)

INDEX OF ROUTES

SCOTTISH MOUNTAINEERING CLUB
SCOTTISH MOUNTAINEERING TRUST

Prices were correct at time of publication, but are subject to change

CLIMBERS' GUIDES

Ben Nevis	£20.00
Glen Coe	£20.00
Lowland Outcrops	£20.00
North-East Outcrops	£20.00
Northern Highlands North	£20.00
Northern Highlands Central	£20.00
Scottish Rock Climbs	£21.00
Arran, Arrochar and Southern Highlands	£15.00
The Cairngorms Vols. 1/2	£11.00/£12.00
Highland Outcrops	£17.50
Scottish Winter Climbs	£19.00
Skye	£11.00

HILLWALKERS' GUIDES

The Munros	£20.00
The Munros CD-ROM	£40.00
Munros GPS data disk – from SMC website	£10.48
The Corbetts & Other Scottish Hills	£20.00
The Corbetts & Other Scottish Hills CD-ROM	£30.00
North-West Highlands	£22.00
The Cairngorms	£18.00
Central Highlands	£18.00
Islands of Scotland Including Skye	£20.00
Southern Highlands	£17.00
Southern Uplands	In preparation

SCRAMBLERS' GUIDES

Skye Scrambles	£15.50

OTHER PUBLICATIONS

Hostile Habitats – Scotland's Mountain Environment	£16.00
The Munroist's Companion	£16.00
Ben Nevis – Britain's Highest Mountain	£15.00

Visit www.smc.org.uk for more details and to purchase on line.

Distributed by: **Cordee Ltd, 3a De Montfort Street, Leicester LE1 7HD**
www.cordee.co.uk   (t) 0116 254 3579   (f) 0116 247 1176

Geological Map of the Northe

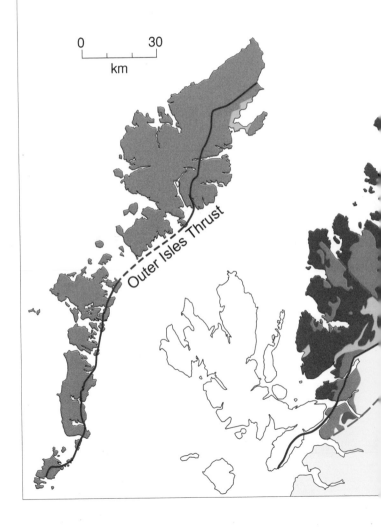

Outer Isles Thrust